Anti-Partisan

Mark Ressler

INCREASINGLY SKEPTICAL PUBLICATIONS

©2025 by Mark Ressler.

All rights reserved.

ISBN 978-1-940551-02-9 (HB)
ISBN 978-1-940551-22-7 (PB)
ISBN 978-1-940551-42-5 (PDF)

Contents

Preface   5

I   **Main Argument**   13

1   Introduction   15

2   On the Abolition of All Political Parties Revisited   29

3   Realignment of Functions of Political Parties   61

4   Elections without Political Parties   91

5   The New Legislators   107

6   Conclusion   123

II   **Topics**   133

7   Partisanship in Philosophy   135

8   Natural Slavery and Partisanship   141

9   Allegedly Wasted Votes   147

10   The Irrelevance of Ideology   153

11   Democracy According to Follett   157

12   General Will, not Necessarily According to Rousseau   169

13   Rights and Responsibilities   179

14 Anarchism and the Value of Unattainable Ideals	187
15 Organizing Without Organizations	193
16 On the Possibility of Taming Organizations	197
References	203

Preface

My elementary school also served as the local polling place for elections. For what passed as civics education at my school, we would occasionally be herded down into the basement where the voting machines were kept to be instructed on how elections worked. At that time, the voting machines were very large machines standing as tall as an adult, as I recall, with curtains that could be pulled around one to keep one's vote confidential. On the front of the machine was an array of levers associated with a candidate running for an elected office, and one voted for a candidate by pulling a lever down.

What particularly caught my attention about these machines were two levers near the top of the machines, one labeled something like "Vote all Democratic Party" and the other "Vote all Republican Party". Pulling one of these levers would automatically pull all of the levers associated with candidates of the corresponding political party. I clearly recall at the time thinking, "Why would anyone pull either of those two levers? Why should I think that all members of a particular political party were worthy of my vote? What if one of them was a complete scoundrel? Shouldn't I always consider each candidate individually?"[1]

This seems to have been my very first independent political thought. I have not changed my mind since then.

I am not now nor have I ever been a member of *any* political party.

When I first registered to vote, I hesitated at the part of the

---

[1] Ostrogorski refers to the practice of withholding vote from one or more candidates on a party ticket by the term "scratching" according to the parlance of late 19th century party politics in the United States (Ostrogorski, 1902b, p. 354). See also (Ostrogorski, 1902b, p. 447–449) for a strategic application of this practice in a faction of one political party.

registration form where I was supposed to indicate my political party affiliation. There I saw options for the two major political parties, as well as an array of third parties, some of which I had never heard of prior to that point. Trying to decide how I was going to respond to this question on the registration form, my attention was briefly drawn to the American Independent Party, but I quickly decided that this option did not adequately describe my political affiliation at all. If they were truly independent, then why did they form a political party? At the very end, there was the option "Decline to state". This too seemed an inadequate description of my political position. It is not that I had an affiliation to a political party, but that I was too shy or ashamed to admit to such an affiliation. Rather I had no affiliation with any party at all and did not want any such affiliation. However, of the available options, that was the least incorrect one, so I selected it. As I moved to different states and communities and registered to vote again, this option always seemed to be the best one presented to me concerning political affiliation: "Decline to state" or sometimes simply abbreviated as "DTS". The option I truly wanted to see was "Rejects all political parties".

I have voted for members of a variety of different political parties over the years, often subsequently regretting my vote as the elected candidate for whom I voted ultimately proved to be unworthy of that vote. Eventually, I came to favor candidates who did not run as members of any political party, but I realized that lack of party affiliation was not itself a sufficient condition for meriting my vote. When given the option, I started writing in my own name if there was no candidate that I felt I could support, in one case actually winning an election where the only option was for a write-in candidate. Apparently, no one else besides me wrote in a candidate's name. Failing a write-in option for most candidates in recent elections, I found myself simply leaving my ballot for those positions blank. What I really wished to see was an option "None of the above" by which I could indicate that I was dissatisfied with all of the candidates offered on the ballot and that none of them deserved my vote.[2]

According to the definition of a vote as codified in the laws

---

[2] Some would argue that this option would simply "waste my vote". As I will argue in Chapter 9 below, I think that this style of argument is merely an attempt to coerce my vote, and that there are no wasted votes, even blank votes.

of the state in which I live, leaving my ballot blank means that I have not in fact cast a vote at all. However, setting this legal definition aside, insofar as a vote can be considered an explicit choice regarding candidates in an election, my blank ballot for particular offices does indeed constitute a choice not to accept any of the candidates offered for the office. Accordingly, I do not consider that my vote is being counted, since the election officials in my state do not report how many ballots were blank for each office, only how many ballots were cast for the candidates. Even if reporting the number of blank ballots did not affect the determination of the outcome of the election, I wonder whether more voters would likewise leave their ballots blank for certain offices if it could be tallied and reported as an explicit rejection of the candidates on the ballot. If the number of blank ballots is sufficiently high, such reporting would show that the method for selecting candidates was inadequate, and insofar as candidates are selected by the machinations of political parties, for the most part, the inadequacies of political parties would likewise be more apparent.

Yet elections are only the start of the problem, since inadequate candidates lead to inadequate governance once one of those candidates is actually elected to an office. Where those candidates are nominated by political parties, they tend to stay aligned to those political parties while in office, and political parties have various methods for ensuring that elected officials continue to follow the party line, even in cases where those parties are highly decentralized. In this way, governance becomes polluted by partisan politics, directed not toward solving problems but toward gaining power for the party and ensuring that the party stays in power.

One reaction to the recognition of the problem of partisan politics would be to seek *bi-partisan* or more generally *multi-partisan* solutions to various issues. Yet this reaction aims for consensus among the adherents of various political parties, so even if such consensus were possible regarding certain issues, it would leave the partisan structures in place where they may prove problematic again for other issues.

Another reaction would be to seek explicitly *non-partisan* solutions, attempting to find a method to resolve an issue that somehow is independent of the machinations of political parties. Yet this reaction is scarcely an improvement over the multi-partisan reaction. Assuming that such a non-partisan solution may be available for some issue, the political parties remain in place, ready to assert themselves again at the earliest opportunity.

Consequently, my reaction is to go straight to the core of the problem and to adopt an explicitly *anti-partisan* approach.

My previous book on technology had identified two factors affecting the possibility of an authentic relationship with technology, namely organizations and the cognitive impacts of using technology (Ressler, 2024). This book is an exploration of one instance of the first factor. In considering how to counteract the impacts of organizations, a fundamental question to ask is whether those organizations are necessary at all. If they are not, then perhaps the best way to counteract their impacts is simply to dispense with them entirely.

One type of organization that seems clearly dispensable, at least to non-religious people, is churches. Even for religious people, it might be asked why the relation between people and a deity needs to be mediated at all, and if it is mediated, why that mediation needs to take the form of an organization such as a church. An exploration of this question might ultimately take the form of an extended commentary on Ivan Karamazov's story of the Grand Inquisitor in Dostoyevesky's *The Brothers Karamazov*.

With regard to nations and states, the case is less clear, despite the passionate arguments that have been offered in favor of anarchism.[3] While it might be acknowledged that specific nations are too invasive into the lives and choices of the people within their realms, the lack of any permanent, organized government would seem to open an opportunity for particular individuals to oppress and to take advantage of others, although it may be the case that arguments in favor of anarchism simply have not yet articulated the proper mechanisms by which nations and states might be abolished without enabling oppression of the weak by the strong.

Likewise, the case of businesses and corporations is unclear, particularly since it seems that the large population of people at present can no longer be provided with necessary goods and services without the economies of scale that organizations in the form of businesses and corporations provide. This does not mean that

---

[3] See Chapter 14 for reflections on the ideal of anarchism.

corporations need to be tolerated in their current forms, since there seem to be definite problems that can be identified with corporations that might be amenable to some correction and control, but it may indeed be the case that corporations constitute a necessary evil in modern society.

If I were exclusively interested in the problems related to technology, it would seem that exploring organizations in the form of businesses and corporations in greater detail would have been more appropriate in this study, since these kinds of organizations appear to have a more direct impact on the direction in which technology expands and therefore have a greater technological impact on people than any other kind of organization. However, a number of reasons induced me to write instead about organizations in the form of political parties:

1. The metaphor of a *political machine* makes the exploration of political parties following a study of technology particularly attractive. Originally applied to organizations like Tammany Hall in the United States in the 19th century, the metaphor has outlived the existence of such flagrant instances of political machines, though it seems that similar political machinery still exists in less blatant forms. A sense of powerlessness to influence the course of politics in the shadow of such political machinery provides an compelling parallel to a feeling of helplessness in the face of technological expansion.

2. As I described above, I have never been a member or an adherent of any political party, and I was acutely coming to a realization that political parties did not merely fail properly to represent me politically, but that they were in fact an adverse factor in the proper governance of the country in which I lived, as well as in other countries.

3. By chance, I discovered Simone Weil's *On the Abolition of All Political Parties* (Weil, 2014), which advanced my thinking on political parties even further, pushing me from a non-partisan to an anti-partisan stance, and prompting me to consider how a democratic country might be governed without any political parties whatsoever.

4. The political situation in my country was becoming increasingly dysfunctional, in a way that further confirmed my suspicions concerning the adverse impacts of political parties. This dysfunction effectively raised the stakes of this line of philosophical and political thought for me. It was not merely a question of my personal political orientation, but a vital question affecting the governance of an entire country and thereby affecting the course of history.

Thus, this book began to take shape in its current form even as I was working to complete the book on technology. The chapter structure of the main argument in Part I flowed naturally from the identification of the problem, from the arguments that Weil and others have presented as well as those that I was in the process of formulating, and from the need to think through alternatives for elections and governance if indeed political parties were abolished as Weil recommends.

The argument in this book is that political parties are one kind of organization that no longer serve people well, if they ever did, and that they can be abolished in favor of other institutions or mechanisms for accomplishing political goals within a modern democracy. Whether other organizations are similarly dispensable will require further thought and argument.

Besides the work by Weil, my reading has uncovered other works challenging political parties, including the extensive study on political parties by Moisei Ostrogorski, which has become quite dated by now, covering less than half of the history of modern political parties. I have not found many studies that consolidated previous arguments against political parties particularly well, except interestingly for a book in support of political parties.[4] Nor have I found many sustained arguments for how all the functions of political parties might be served in other ways if political parties were abolished, though there are numerous proposals for alternative institutions for specific functions. Thus I could not find any comprehensive book against political parties, which I thought should already be available, prompting me to write the book myself, as was the case with the book on technology.

This book is the second in a projected three part series in applied philosophy, with the first book arguing for an authentic en-

---

[4](Rosenblum, 2010).

gagement with technology, identifying two factors that compromise such an authentic relationship. This second book argues against a particular instance of the first factor, namely organizations in the form of political parties. The third projected book will develop considerations concerning the second factor, namely the cognitive impacts of using technology. In particular, it will investigate the suggestion in the book on technology that existing ethical theories are fundamentally grounded in technological thinking, and it will apply these considerations to problems in a specific branch of applied philosophy, namely environmental philosophy.

Although I am strongly inclined toward perspectival thinking and methodology, evidenced by the structure of the book on technology, in which the relationship between people and technology was considered in both directions, this study firmly takes a stance within a single perspective, namely a position against political parties. While I will consider objections to the arguments against political parties, as any responsible work of philosophy should, this book represents the culmination of decades of personal political reflection starting with my childhood reaction to the partisan levers on voting machines as described above. I could attempt to present this study within a perspectival framework, but that would not seem to be completely honest, since I have never approached this particular issue in any other manner than from deep skepticism and suspicion concerning political parties, unlike other philosophical issues on which I have remained undecided. Consequently, it seems to me that it would be more forthright simply to be open about the perspective from which I approach the issue and not to adopt a pretense of perspectival thinking.

The same two-part structure that appeared in the book on technology is also adopted here, namely to keep the main argument focused within the first part, then to offer a second part on additional topics that are related but not necessary to that argument.

Part I

Main Argument

Chapter 1

Introduction

E. E. Schattschneider claims "that modern democracy is unthinkable save in terms of the parties" (Schattschneider, 2017, p. 1). Yet the inability of one or even a large number of people to conceive an alternative does not prove that democracy without political parties is unthinkable.[1] It suffices for one person to demonstrate an alternative to falsify Schattschneider's claim. Such is one aim of this book, namely to explore the possibility of alternatives to political parties within modern democracies in all of their functions.

John H. Aldrich concludes his evaluation of political parties with the statement: "In America democracy is unthinkable save in terms of a two-party system, because no collection of ambitious politicians has long been able to think of a way to achieve their goals in this democracy save in terms of political parties" (Aldrich, 2001, p. 323). Yet a democracy does not exist fundamentally in order for ambitious politicians to achieve their goals. Nor should it be surprising that such politicians will not have found an alternative solution, since it may be doubted whether they are even looking for such an alternative. Perhaps one should not look to politicians for alternative ways in which democracy may be conducted, if they are mainly seeking to achieve their own goals, however much they may protest that their goals coincide with the good of the community or nation. There would seem to be an opportunity here for others besides politicians, perhaps even a philosopher, to consider

---

[1]Yet writers persist in invoking some form of unthinkability, for example, "Parties ...do so much work, in fact, that it is nearly impossible to imagine democratic government functioning in their absence" (Muirhead, 2014, p. 7).

the actual value that political parties provide to democracies.

Hans Kelsen goes further than invoking mere unthinkability and claims, "Only self-deception or hypocrisy could lead one to suppose that democracy is possible without political parties. A democratic state is necessarily and unavoidably a multiparty state" (Kelsen, 2013, p. 39).[2] However, assertions concerning the necessity of political parties tend not to be accompanied by any supporting arguments, and indeed Kelsen does not provide any such argument. In fact, I have yet to see any argument for the necessity of political parties that comes close to the structure of an argument in accordance with the logic of necessity. Worse still, Kelsen engages in the fallacy of poisoning the well by his imputation of self-deception and hypocrisy to those who disagree with him.[3]

Following Richard Hofstadter (Hofstadter, 1969, pp. 16–33), one might epitomize the attitudes toward political parties according to the positions of three important 18th century thinkers:

Henry Bolingbroke — opposition: "*party* is a political evil, and *faction* is the *worst* of all *parties*" (Bolingbroke, 1749, p. 140).

David Hume — tolerance: "To exclude faction from a free government is very difficult, if not altogether impracticable" (Hume, 1987, p. 407).

Edmund Burke — endorsement: "Party divisions, whether on the whole operating for good or evil, are things inseparable from free government" (Burke, 1769, p. 1).

While these attitudes may still be applicable to modern political parties in a logical or schematic manner, the exact arguments of these thinkers cannot simply be extended to modern political parties, since the parties or factions to which the original arguments were directed are not the same as modern political parties in their nature and organization. Indeed, it seems that these thinkers could scarcely have predicted what political parties would become in the 19th and 20th centuries and beyond.

---

[2] Likewise, according to Richard Rose, "political parties are a necessary, important and imperfect feature of British government today" (Rose, 1974, p. 1).

[3] Nor will this be the only instance of gross logical fallacies in arguments against those who propose the abolition of political parties encountered within the course of this book. See Section 3.7.

Consequently, it seems necessary at the outset of this study to note the various conceptions and definitions of factions and parties that have been proposed before discussing any previous arguments regarding their relative evils or merits. For example:

Faction "The acceptation in which the term [faction] is generally used is that of a seditious party in the state. The term 'party' in itself implies nothing that is odious, that of faction is always odious" (Voltaire, 1901, p. 322).

"By a faction, I understand a number of citizens, whether amounting to a majority or minority of the whole, who are united and actuated by some common impulse of passion, or of interest, adverse to the rights of other citizen, or to the permanent and aggregate interests of the community" (Hamilton, Madison, & Jay, 1788, p. 54).

"That word [faction], in fact, seems to have had the meaning of a more sinister version of 'party' — party functioning at its worst. ...It was only in a much later period that faction came to mean simply and clearly what it now means to us — a subdivision of a larger party, or a party within a party" (Hofstadter, 1969, pp. 10-11).

"A faction is a highly cohesive group that cuts the party vertically" (Panebianco, 1988, p. 74).

"*factions* (specific power groups within [a party])" (Ware, 1996, p. 109).

Party "Parties, even before they degenerate into absolute factions, are still numbers of men associated together for certain purposes, and certain interests, which are not, or which are not allowed to be, those of the community by others" (Bolingbroke, 1749, p. 130).

"Party is a body of men united, for promoting by their joint endeavours the national interest, upon some particular principle in which they are all agreed" (Burke, 1770, p. 57).

"Party is organized opinion" (Disraeli, 1883, p. 241).

"By a party we understand a number of citizens who, for some period and not momentarily, act in unison respecting some principles, interest, or measure, by lawful means, keeping therefore within the bounds of the fundamental law and for the real or sincerely supposed common good of the whole commonwealth." (Lieber, 1876, p. 253).

"A political party is an organized attempt to get control of the government" (Schattschneider, 2017, p. lix).

"...present-day parties are distinguished far less by their programme or the class of members than by the nature of their organization. A party is a community with a particular structure" (Duverger, 1964, p. xv).

"Almost everything that is called a party in any Western democratic nation can be so regarded for the present purpose. This means any group, however loosely organized, seeking to elect governmental office-holders under a given label" (Epstein, 1967, p. 9).

"A political party is an organization concerned with the expression of popular preferences and contesting control of the chief policy-making offices of government" (Rose, 1974, p. 3).

"A party is any political group identified by an official label that presents at elections, and is capable of placing through elections (free or non-free), candidates for public office" (Sartori, 2005, p. 56).

"A political party is an institution that *(a)* seeks influence in a state, often by attempting to occupy positions in government, and *(b)* usually consists of more than a single interest in the society and so to some degree attempts to 'aggregate interests' (Ware, 1996, p. 5).

As can be seen from these few samples of definitions, the distinction between factions and parties has shifted over time. Additionally, many of these definitions are loaded in favor of the arguments for or against political parties on the part of the definer.[4]

---

[4]Additionally, Ostrogorski refers to Alexander Pope's definition of a party (Ostrogorski, 1902b, p. 572), but what is quoted is actually Pope's characterization of "party-spirit, which at best is but the madness of many for the gain of a few" (Pope, 1824, p. 348). As will be seen in Section 3.7, some recent writers make a distinction between partisanship and adherence to political parties, where party spirit might be understood differently according to either side of this distinction.

It is no longer clear that it is argumentatively useful to maintain even the old connotations between factions as bad and parties as good, given the shift in meaning over time.[5] Where early factions had become problematic, it seems understandable that some would seek a new term to describe associations of people that are not problematic in the same way as those factions. "Party" was chosen as this new term. Very well. Yet what those parties later became does not clearly honor any previous distinctions, but rather seems exactly as problematic as early factions. Attempting to maintain the old connotations between factions and parties risks loading arguments by virtue of mere stipulations and likewise risks equivocation, particularly if the historical distinctions between factions and parties need to be explained to modern citizens in order to make a case for or against political parties. It seems far better to accept the modern usage of the terms and to align any historical arguments to this usage.

Yet for my purposes here, it is insufficient to contrast just factions and parties. Consider the following:

Suppose that there is a question or issue facing a legislature. Inevitably, there will be disagreement concerning this issue, both among members of the legislature and among citizens outside the legislature. Where opinions agree, those sharing the same opinions may consider themselves to be part of some common thing. Call this commonality a *side*. Note that a side is always relative to some question or issue.

Suppose further that those on the same side of that issue within the legislature begin to act together to coordinate their efforts in order to codify their side into law. In this way, they begin to function as a *faction* within the legislature. Note that a faction in this sense is always a part of a broader organization, such as a legislature or a political party, in accordance with more modern usage, as suggested in the quotation on factions from Hofstadter presented above.

The previous supposition posits that the faction arises in order to coordinate action among those on the same side of an issue, but this is not the only way that a faction may arise. Hume calls the

---

[5]Both (Sartori, 2005, pp. 3–12) and (White & Ypi, 2016, pp. 35–39) trace the history of the proposed distinction between factions and parties, and White and Ypi still try to make the distinction relevant (White & Ypi, 2016, p. 188), unsuccessfully in my opinion.

kind of faction arising from a side of a question a *real* faction, since it is "founded on some real difference of sentiment or interest", but he also recognizes factions "founded on personal friendship or animosity" (Hume, 1987, p. 56). Furthermore, "*Real* factions may be divided into those from *interest*, from *principle*, and from *affection*" (Hume, 1987, p. 59). Yet however a faction may arise within a legislature, it is immaterial to the discussion here, so long as that faction is recognized as constituting a part of a broader organization.

Next suppose that the members of this faction decide to continue to act together, not just to coordinate legislation for the original question or issue, but to do so for any number of future issues. In order to coordinate better among themselves within the legislature, they form an organization with certain defined roles and offices, including procedures to fill those offices when individual members retire or fail to be re-elected to the legislature. Call this organization a *caucus*. Note that a caucus in this sense both exists within a broader organization, namely the legislature, and exists as an organization in its own right.

Finally, suppose that members of this caucus extend their organization outside of the legislature, in order to coordinate action not only within the legislature in question, but also within other levels of government, whether national, regional, or local, whether executive, legislative, or judicial. In order to coordinate effectively, this extended organization seeks to influence elections such that elected officials at all levels and in all roles act in concert with regard to whatever questions and issues arise. Call this organization a *political party*.

A political party may arise in a different way than suggested here, possibly even independently of a pre-existing caucus or faction or even side of an issue, though it will most probably emerge from at least one of these.[6] For the purposes of this discussion, it is immaterial how the party emerges, so long as that party constitutes an organization that seeks to influence other organizations and institutions, particularly legislatures and other governmental

---

[6]Sartori understands faction to be a sub-unit of party (Sartori, 2005, p. 64), but I think Sartori is taking the perspective of a political party too strongly, where faction can be understood in a broader sense. Aldrich considers it "reasonable to conclude that parties arose out of the step-by-step strengthening of factions into political parties" (Aldrich, 2001, p. 94), congenially to my presentation here.

		Constitutes an organization	
		No	Yes
Within an organization	No	Side	Political Party
	Yes	Faction	Caucus

Table 1.1: Categorization of groups related to Political Parties

offices, especially by means of elections affecting the composition of those offices.

These four kinds of groups, side, faction, caucus, and political party, may accordingly be categorized across two dimensions:

1. Whether the group is a part of a broader organization

2. Whether the group itself constitutes an organization

Table 1.1 summarizes this categorization.

As cited above, Hume thought that "To exclude faction from a free government is very difficult, if not altogether impracticable" (Hume, 1987, p. 407). Indeed, it is not my intention to argue against factions or sides, as characterized here. These seem inevitable. Even if an organization is created specifically from groups of people who think the same way on a given issue, it seems that there will eventually be some other issue on which they disagree, leading to the formation of factions within that organization. Indeed, this level of disagreement seems healthy within a democracy.[7]

Rather, the target of this study is political parties and to some extent caucuses, insofar as they share the same tendencies as political parties. What is common to these two, unlike sides or factions, is that they themselves constitute organizations. The argument in

---

[7]The diatribes against factions in the early history of the United States, as epitomized in Washington's Farewell address (Washington, 1919), for example, as will be summarized in Section 2.2, thus seem a bit naive, as though it should be expected that just because a group of people agree to form a new nation, they should be expected to agree on all other issues that may arise within that nation. These complaints against factions are perhaps best re-construed retrospectively in terms of political parties, which were then in the early stages of development, rather than mere factions in the sense presented here.

this book will be that these organizations tend not to serve people fundamentally, but tend to make people serve them in order to obtain power and to remain in power.

Some of the arguments will apply to pressure groups as well, which are likewise organizations, but seem to function as a hybrid between a side and a political party, and therefore do not fit cleanly within the categorization in Table 1.1. So long as a pressure group functions more as a side, rather than a political party, the arguments in this book will not properly apply to it.[8]

One may object at this point, even without hearing the arguments against political parties and related organizations, that people have a fundamental right to organize among themselves in order to achieve their social and political goals. Political parties and pressure groups are merely the result of this right to organize; consequently, any arguments that compromise this right must ultimately be faulty and unjust.

Yet this objection relies on a false consequence. Just because people have a right to *organize* among themselves does not necessarily mean that *organizations* have a right to exist and to persist. Organizations constitute an ontological category above the mere group of people who are members of that organization, as noted in the book on technology.[9] When people organize themselves to coordinate action to achieve a goal, that itself does not bring an organization into existence. A group of people coordinating action among themselves may remain a mere group without forming an organization. By contrast, an organization must have persistent roles that continue to be filled when a previous occupant of that role ceases to serve in that role, such that the organization can continue as the same organization even when the original people who created the organization no longer exist.[10]

Nor do the arguments in this book conclude that all political organizations must therefore be abolished, such as pressure groups. Suppose that a group of people organize themselves to achieve some political goal, and suppose that they not only coordinate actions among themselves but that they also create an organization, perhaps to perform fundraising within the bounds of politi-

---

[8] On pressure groups, see (Key, 1942) and (Epstein, 1967, p. 12).

[9] (Ressler, 2024, pp. 57–59).

[10] See Chapter 15 for more reflections on organizing and organizations in relation to this objection.

cal finance laws. Suppose further that the organization achieves its goal, upon which the organization is disbanded. In this case, the arguments in this book will not apply to such an organization.

If, however, upon the achievement of its goal, the organization decides to persist in order to achieve additional goals, then the pressure group begins to function more like a political party, and some of the arguments in this book will apply to it, though not necessarily all of the arguments. Similarly with regard to a caucus. Therefore, with regard to any political organization, the nature and function of that organization would need to be evaluated against the specific arguments presented in Chapter 2. I claim that modern political parties run afoul of all the arguments presented there.

One may further object that these arguments are fundamentally undemocratic, since political parties have been necessary to the development of modern democracies, as claimed by Schattschneider and others in the quotations at the beginning of this chapter. Of course, democracies have existed in some form prior to the development of modern democracies, notably in the first instances of democracies of ancient Greece. While sides and factions were common among those early democracies, political parties had not yet emerged, so political parties are clearly not necessary to every form of democracy.

Yet besides the inapplicability of the objection to democracy in its earliest forms, it should be noted that this objection likewise relies on false consequences. Even if I were to agree that political parties were instrumental to the development of specifically modern democracies, even necessary to such development, that does not mean that political parties are still necessary to the continued operation of those democracies, or to the creation of new democracies. The circumstances in which modern democracies formerly developed are not the same circumstances as at the present time. Two aspects are particularly notable in this context:

1. *Communications.* Where communications technologies were restricted at the time that modern democracies first developed, limiting the ability of citizens to follow and to understand the issues that were relevant at the time, the varieties and speed of modern communications technologies have greatly increased since then.

2. *Literacy.* Where low levels of literacy at the time that mod-

ern democracies developed limited the ability of citizens to use the print media that was available, literacy levels and education levels in general have significantly risen since then, such that a broader range of citizens is able to read and to evaluate political arguments in a way that was not previously possible.

Consequently, the three 18th century attitudes toward political parties noted at the beginning of this chapter, exemplified by Bolingbroke, Hume, and Burke, are not exhaustive of the possible attitudes. In particular, one may indeed acknowledge the debt that modern democracies owe to political parties in the early development of those democracies, but also to recognize that political parties are no longer necessary, and indeed may now represent factors that compromise democracy. Perhaps some new democracies may still require political parties in order to help those democracies become established, particularly if their levels of communications and literacy are not sufficiently high, but once the democracies become established, those political parties may become harmful relics of an early stage of development and should therefore be discarded. Thus, it is not fundamentally undemocratic to argue against modern political parties.

The presentation of the arguments against political parties in Chapter 2 begins with the arguments offered by Simone Weil in her short work *On the Abolition of All Political Parties* (Weil, 2014). Her arguments were not universally well received at the time, written in the middle of the Second World War and published after her death, upon which some rejected her arguments on the unsupportable supposition that only political parties can prevent Fascism from arising again, whereas the Fascism that led to the war was enabled precisely by political parties. Even decades later, one of Weil's otherwise sympathetic biographers would refer to the abolition of political parties as "this fundamentally undemocratic concept" (Gray, 2001, p. 201).

Where Weil went wrong, it seems, is only arguing for the abolition of political parties. In order for the arguments to be accepted, one must also argue for how democracies can operate without political parties. In particular, one must show that the functions that political parties have served within democracies either can be served in other ways once political parties have been abolished, or that those functions need not be served at all. This is the task of Chapter 3.

Furthermore, one must argue how members of those democracies can continue to act democratically once political parties have been abolished. In particular, how will citizens vote and how will legislators make laws without the mediation of political parties? These questions will be explored in Chapters 4 and 5, respectively.

This strategy can be generalized into a formula for evaluating whether other types or organizations, such as corporations or states, are necessary or whether they too can be abolished:

- Evaluate whether the organizations cause definite harm to people.

- Determine whether the functions of those organizations can be served in other ways or whether those functions need to be served at all.

- Explore how people in various roles can continue to achieve their goals without those organizations.

This book, though, focuses on just one kind of organization, namely political parties. The overall argument is that political parties no longer serve people in the ways that they had been intended to serve, but now seek to influence people to serve their own goals, and therefore that political parties should be abolished.

The arguments against political parties that I add to those provided by Weil, Ostrogorski, and others are grounded in the idea of *political inauthenticity*. The book on technology developed the idea of authenticity as contrasted with the notion of genuineness, where being genuine as opposed to being a fake is concerned with correct attribution of identity, for example, being a genuine human person rather than a mechanical robot that cleverly simulates a human person. Being authentic as opposed to being inauthentic concerns whether one is acting as an individual rather than as a mere arbitrary representative of some group.[11]

---

[11] (Ressler, 2024, p. 85). Some have found the use of the term 'authenticity' in the book on technology problematic, preferring to have the notion characterized by some other term, whether because it represents philosophical jargon necessitating a distinction from the ordinary sense of genuineness, or because it was too closely associated with Heidegger, whom they hold to be objectionable. Indeed,

The book on technology analyzed authenticity primarily in terms of group membership and dynamics, rather than following earlier philosophical attempts at understanding authenticity in terms of various abstractions, such as *the public*, a *herd*, or merely some shadowy indistinct *they*. Political inauthenticity can be understood in accordance with this analysis.

Suppose that I am a member of some political party. Do I value everything that the party values, judge everything in accordance with the party's decisions, and endorse every action that the party takes? If so, that does not immediately indicate that I am exhibiting political inauthenticity. It may happen that these are the values I would have held, the judgements that I would have made, and the actions that I would have endorsed if the political party did not exist.

Suppose now that I were a member of a different political party. Would I now value everything that *this* party values, judge everything in accordance with *this* party's decisions, and endorse every action that *this* party takes? If so, this suggests that my values, judgements, and actions fundamentally align to whatever political party or organization to which I happen to belong, rather than representing a case in which my party membership represents a choice reflecting my values, judgements, and desired actions. As such, this exemplifies what I mean by political inauthenticity, though as noted in the book on technology, authenticity and inauthenticity are not absolute, but may be manifest in degrees.[12]

My arguments against political parties are intended to demonstration that political parties tend to encourage precisely this pattern of political inauthenticity, and thereby tend to undermine individual political choice, which is essential to a healthy democracy.

Indeed, I am assuming in what follows that the evaluation of political parties is being conducted within the context of a modern democracy. In a totalitarian regime, for example, it seems to me

---

it might have been preferable to have some other term to describe the concern that seems to be common to Kierkegaard, Nietzsche, and Heidegger, but I think there is sense in which the term 'authenticity' captures this notion perfectly well, without risking the inelegance of some awkward neologism. Authenticity in this sense indicates that one is acting as a *genuine* individual, rather than an otherwise interchangeable member of some group who values, judges, and acts in the same way as any other member of that group.

[12](Ressler, 2024, pp. 87–90).

that it matters very little whether the totalitarianism supports one political party, several of them, or none at all. The fundamental problem in that case is the pattern of totalitarianism, not the role of political parties. Rather, it is within democracies that political parties themselves become problematic.

Consider Duverger's simple definition of democracy: "a regime in which those who govern are chosen by those who are governed, by means of free and open elections" (Duverger, 1964, p. 353).[13] Political parties do not feature in this definition, not even as a logical consequence. Indeed, Duverger notes in his conclusion that "The organization of political parties is certainly not in conformity with orthodox notions of democracy" (Duverger, 1964, p. 422). Rather, political parties represent third parties between those who are governed and those who govern them.[14]

The fundamental question, then, is whether democracies need to be mediated by political parties. I believe they do not, and I am prepared to argue for that conclusion.

---

[13]Although Duverger later questions this definition (Duverger, 1964, pp. 423–424), as will be discussed in the Conclusion.

[14]Schattschneider makes a troubling claim: "The parties occupy a blind spot in the theory of democracy just as they occupy a zone unknown to the law. The only way to discover the parties is to revise the definition of democracy" (Schattschneider, 2017, p. 15). If taken seriously, this suggestion opens arguments in favor of political parties to charges of logical fallacy, if the definition of democracy has been engineered specifically to support the necessity of political parties.

Chapter 2

On the Abolition of All Political Parties Revisited

Previous arguments against political parties have apparently been so varied and numerous that one author offers the following categorization of such arguments:

- "Assessments of the first type hold electoral system rules and/or legislative traditions responsible for the relevant problem with the parties" (Scarrow, 1996, p. 301).

- "A second variety of anti-party argument blames the current spectrum of party alternatives for creating the observed deficiencies" (Scarrow, 1996, p. 301).

- "Finally, a third variety of causal argument blames fundamental aspects of the political system for assigning parties inappropriate tasks" (Scarrow, 1996, p. 302).

Yet interestingly this author omits a category that identifies the problems of political parties in their very nature as organizations, rather than shifting the blame to some factor other than the nature of political parties themselves. It is these kinds of arguments that will be particularly important for the purposes of this book. If the problem with political parties rests primarily with electoral systems or legislative traditions, then those systems and traditions might be changed. If the problem rests primarily with the spectrum of party alternatives, then new alternatives might be presented. If the problem rests primarily with the political system, then that political system might be amended. In any of these cases, the problems with political parties might be alleviated in order for them more properly to serve the functions for which they were devised. However, if the problem with political parties rests primarily in their nature as organizations, then political parties are fundamentally problematic, and the solution would seem to be that they should be abolished.

Simone Weil adopts precisely this strategy, so I start by revisiting her arguments.

2.1 Weil's Argument

Weil's *On the Abolition of All Political Parties* reads somewhat ironically like a pamphlet from a political party in its tone, whether accidentally or intentionally. Yet rather than engaging in mere antipartisan rhetoric, Weil employs a clear argumentative structure to reach her conclusion that political parties should be abolished.

After extolling Rousseau's conception of the general will and identifying two conditions whereby the notion of the general will can be applied (Weil, 2014, pp. 5–11),[1] Weil claims three characteristics of political parties that will serve as a framework for evaluating the extent to which they are conducive to "truth, justice, and the public interest":

1. A political party is a machine to generate collective passions.
2. A political party is an organisation designed to exert collective pressure upon the minds of all its individual members.
3. The first objective and also the ultimate goal of any political party is its own growth, without limit. (Weil, 2014, p. 11)

Weil considers these characteristics in the reverse order.

With regard to the third characteristic, namely the goal of unlimited growth for the party, Weil notes that a political party may recognize that in order for it to achieve its goals, it must first secure

---

[1] See Chapter 12 for my own reflections on Rousseau's notion of the general will, which I do not extol.

power, but that it inevitably mistakes the means for an end in itself. "The goal of a political party is something vague and unreal" (Weil, 2014, p. 13), whereas the political party itself is very concrete. Consequently, the material growth of the political party, in terms of the number of members and the amount of donations collected, becomes the sole measure of the success of the party (Weil, 2014, p. 15), in which case there would seem to be no limit to the potential success according to these measures, since there can always be more members recruited and more funds collected.

With regard to the second characteristic, namely the collective pressure exerted on party members, Weil presents this as a consequence of the third characteristic, since in order to continue the unlimited growth of the political party, it must influence peoples' minds (Weil, 2014, pp. 15–16). This influence is allegedly exerted in the form of education according to political parties, but Weil claims that this influence ultimately amounts only to conditioning and propaganda. The discussion of this second characteristic represents the bulk of Weil's argument.

Weil notes that it becomes natural for people to speak relative to party positions, namely "as a conservative" or "as a Socialist" (Weil, 2014, p. 17), therefore encouraging the impression of the relativity of truth itself (Weil, 2014, p. 18). For a member of a party inclined to think independently, that person would thereby be forced to lie in some way, either to the party by virtue of maintaining opinions contrary to the party, or to oneself in professing party opinions that one does not actually hold, or even to the public if that party member is an elected representative obliged to maintain party solidarity in government in contrast to the personal opinions that the member holds (Weil, 2014, pp. 19–20).

Political parties impose discipline on their members to ensure conformity of opinions, such as the mechanisms that the Communist party developed to impact adversely all aspects of the lives of those who are insubordinate to the dictates of the party, including penalties affecting "career, affections, friendship, reputation, the external aspect of honour, sometimes even family life" (Weil, 2014, p. 22). Weil notes that it was the Church that initially introduced these mechanisms to combat heresy, relying on the great profusion of articles of faith, not all of which Church members can be aware, in order to foster a level of dependence on the authority of the Church (Weil, 2014, pp. 25-26). Similarly, someone joining a political party cannot be aware of all the positions that the party has adopted, so ultimately the authority of the party becomes paramount (Weil, 2014, p. 27).

Yet these external penalties ultimately become internalized such that discipline is not even required. Weil introduces a thought experiment whereby someone is required to perform complex numerical computations, but that person is beaten every time the results of the computations are even numbers. In such a case, Weil notes that this person would be likely "to give a slight twist to the calculations, in order to obtain an odd number in the end" (Weil, 2014, p. 23). Likewise, the threat of external discipline by political parties conditions party members to accept the authority of the party. This conditioning encourages one to think primarily as a party member, accepting the positions and dictates of the political party, such that ultimately, "Nothing is more comfortable than not having to think" (Weil, 2014, p. 27).

With regard to the first characteristic, namely the generation of collective passions, Weil simply claims that "this is so spectacularly evident that it scarcely needs further demonstration" (Weil, 2014, p. 28), apparently thinking that support for this characteristic follows directly from the discussion of the second one, since the collective pressures that political parties exert are not conducive to rational reflection on the part of its members, so they must thereby generate passions instead. Weil draws an analogy with intoxicating drugs, which are prohibited, whereas the similar effects of political parties on the minds of people are actually condoned by the state.

In arguing for these three characteristics of political parties, Weil simultaneously demonstrates that these characteristics are not conducive to truth, justice, and the public interest. These characteristics are in fact the characteristics of totalitarianism, leading Weil to conclude that "the institution of political parties appears to be an almost unmitigated evil. They are bad in principle, and in practice their impact is noxious. The abolition of parties would prove almost wholly beneficial" (Weil, 2014, p. 28).

On reviewing Weil's argument, while there is much that is persuasive and even compelling in the argument, it must be acknowledged that the argument is fundamentally incomplete. First, Weil seems to be focused primarily on the phenomenology of party membership and its effects on the inner experience of individuals, without investigating the external impacts of political parties.

2.1. WEIL'S ARGUMENT

The impact of political parties on elections is another aspect where the influence of political parties might be evaluated, for example. Likewise, since most political parties seek to influence elections in order to place representatives and executives in office to enact policies and legislation favorable to the party, the impact of political parties on the governance process ought to be explored as well. While the influence of political parties on individuals may indeed serve to demonstrate that they are not conducive to truth and justice, in order to demonstrate that they are not conducive to the public interest, it would seem necessary to evaluate the influence of political parties on elections and governance where the public interest intersects most with political parties. Weil does not consider these aspects in any significant detail.

Second, by focusing strictly on three *characteristics* that Weil imputes to political parties, Weil does not consider all of the *functions* that political parties serve within a state or a community. It may be that some of these functions are actually beneficial, despite the adverse impacts of the characteristics for which Weil argues, in which case Weil cannot properly claim that political parties are an "unmitigated evil". Perhaps they are evil, but that evil may in fact be mitigated by some useful functions that political parties serve, perhaps that they uniquely serve. Yet if political parties do serve some beneficial functions, then the question that should be raised is whether those benefits outweigh the detrimental impacts that Weil argues they have. Indeed, Weil herself begins her presentation in a way that suggests that she would conduct such a comparative evaluation: "The evils of political parties are all too evident; therefore, the problem that should be examined is this: do they contain enough good to compensate for their evils and make their preservation desirable?" (Weil, 2014, p. 4). However, Weil fails even to look for any possible good that political parties may provide to a nation or to a community. Consequently, it would seem that Weil's argument simply cannot be accepted as being definitive, but rather provides only one side of an argument that is incomplete in her presentation.

Yet weighing good aspects against bad aspects implies that one can find a common measure and can quantify these aspects in some meaningful way such that one could conclude that political parties are more bad than good. It is not clear that such quantification according to a common measure is even possible. In fact,

Weil rejects such an evaluation of political parties and asks rather, "do they do the slightest bit of good?" (Weil, 2014, p. 4). Weil does not find any such good, but then she does not look very hard for it either.

This chapter will continue this pattern of argument by focusing solely on the problems of political parties. The complete argument against political parties will continue in subsequent chapters, according to the strategy outlined in the Introduction.

2.2 Other Criticisms of Political Parties

Weil was not the first to point out the problems with political parties, so before formulating any new arguments, it will be useful to review some of the key earlier criticisms as well as some subsequent ones. As noted previously, early arguments against parties preceded the development of modern political parties, and therefore more properly apply to factions as characterized in the Introduction. However, I present them here nevertheless, since if these are problems with factions, then they will likely be problems with political parties that develop from factions as well.[2]

Henry Bolingbroke's opposition to political parties derives mainly from his desire for a unified state under a Patriot King, where division of the state by virtue of parties encourages private ambition rather than the overall health of the state (Bolingbroke, 1749, pp. 152–153). When a strong king emerges, Bolingbroke sees parties becoming united which were formerly divided on their opinions concerning government (Bolingbroke, 1735, pp. 4–5). Therefore, the divisions according to political parties represent an undesirable situation within a state. Perhaps it was easy for Bolingbroke to oppose parties, since he could always falls back on the ideal of the Patriot King, whereas democracies without such a monarch must somehow find able and honorable representatives among partisan disputes.

David Hume's criticisms of parties seem to be grounded in the excessive zeal that they foster, whereas Hume prefers moderation (Hume, 1987, p. 27). The consequence of such partisan zeal is that

---

[2] For a more extensive discussion of the history of criticisms of political parties, see (Rosenblum, 2010), although for some reason this large volume neglects even to mention Simone Weil.

2.2. OTHER CRITICISMS OF POLITICAL PARTIES

"Factions subvert government, render laws impotent, and beget the fiercest animosities among men of the same nation, who ought to give mutual assistance and protection to each other" (Hume, 1987, p. 55). Such partisan zeal may lead to the absurd situation in which parties continue to oppose each other after the real difference between them is lost (Hume, 1987, p. 58), for example between the Whig and Tory parties as Hume saw them at the time (Hume, 1987, pp. 69–70).

The authors of the *Federalist Papers*, particularly the author of Number 10, see factions as responsible for "The instability, injustice, and confusion introduced into the public councils", where citizens complain "that the public good is disregarded in the conflicts of rival parties, and that measures are too often decided, not according to the rules of justice and the rights of the minor party, but by the superior force of an interested and overbearing majority" (Hamilton et al., 1788, p. 53). However, the author claims "that the *causes* of faction cannot be removed, and that relief is only to be sought in the means of controlling its *effects*" (Hamilton et al., 1788, p. 57), in particular by the means afforded by the new Constitution of the United States of America, which the authors were defending.

However sympathetic one might be with the general line of argumentation in *Federalist* 10 and its conclusions, the details of the argument itself are highly questionable, particularly the considerations supporting the claim that a larger federal republic would be better able to control the adverse effects of factions than a confederation of smaller states. These considerations seem based merely on abstract speculation rather than actual experience, which was inevitable, since at the time the proposed form of government was so new that no prior experience of it was available. Yet they also do not anticipate the differences between factions and political parties, by virtue of the organizational structures that political parties embody, in accordance with the distinctions in the Introduction.

In particular, one might challenge the following claims:

- In a larger republic, "if the proportion of fit characters be not less in the large than in the small republic, the former will present a greater option, and consequently a greater probability of a fit choice" (Hamilton et al., 1788, p. 59). This point seems to represent a simple misunderstanding of the nature of probability. If the proportion of fit to unfit characters is the same in a large republic as in a small one, then there are numerically more fit characters in the larger republic, but the probability that a fit character would be elected to office should be same as in a smaller republic, based solely on considerations of population distribution. Yet if governance of a large republic is less attractive to fit characters than in a small republic, then the probability that fit characters would be elected could be smaller in a larger republic. Mere probabilistic mathematics cannot determine the conditions under which persons of good character are more likely to be elected to office.

- Since representatives will be elected by a larger number of voters in a larger republic, "it will be more difficult for unworthy candidates to practise with success the vicious arts by which elections are too often carried" (Hamilton et al., 1788, p. 59). The claim here is that a small number of voters might be fooled by vicious political arts, but somehow a larger number of voter would be resistant to them. Subsequent experience with political machines such as Tammany Hall, newly founded around the time this claim was made, has clearly contradicted this claim. At the peak of the influence of such political machines, the population of the United States was roughly 20 times larger than at the time the *Federalist Papers* were written, with no abatement of the efficacy of vicious political arts.

- In a larger society, with "a greater variety of parties and interests; you make it less probable that a majority of the whole will have a common motive to invade the rights of other citizens; or if such a common motive exists, it will be more difficult for all who feel it to discover their own strength, and to act in unison with each other" (Hamilton et al., 1788, p. 60). The conclusion here may indeed follow, but the premise that a larger society will result in a larger number of parties has not been supported by experience, given the nature of political parties, particularly in the United States. With regard to factions, certainly a larger society may increase the number of divisions and factions, particularly due to regional differences as the population expands over a greater territory, but once political parties as organizations become factors, those divisions and factions tend to become absorbed and consolidated into political parties, as those parties seek to increase their power bases. Here in particular the author of *Federalist* 10 did not anticipate what modern political parties would become.

- "The influence of factious leaders may kindle a flame within their particular States, but will be unable to spread a general conflagration through the other States" (Hamilton et al., 1788, p. 61). This claim seems to presuppose a low level of communication technology, such that factious leaders could count only on local newspapers and word of mouth to publicize their factious principles. Indeed, the *Federalist Papers* were originally published in newspapers in the state of New York, and seem not to have been republished much outside that state. Yet this claim also does not anticipate the abilities of organizations like political parties to exert a wide influence by establishing a network of local organizations in addition to a central organization.

Thus, while the criticisms of factions and parties in *Federalist* 10 still seem relevant to some degree, the arguments for controlling the effects of parties are inadequate, particularly considering how political parties later developed.

George Washington's *Farewell Address* contains a barrage of accusations against factions and parties:

- They tend "to misrepresent the opinions and aims of other districts" (Washington, 1919, p. 15).

- They become "potent engines, by which cunning, ambitious, and unprincipled men, will be enabled to subvert the power of the people, and to usurp for themselves the reins of government" (Washington, 1919, p. 18).

- "The alternate domination of one faction over another, sharpened by the spirit of revenge natural to party dissension ... is itself a frightful despotism," but it also raises the risk that people may "seek security and repose in the absolute power of an individual," namely a dictator (Washington, 1919, p. 21).

- The spirit of party:
    - "serves always to distract the public councils, and enfeeble the public administration";
    - "agitates the community with ill founded jealousies and false alarms";
    - "kindles the animosity of one part against another";
    - "foments occasional riot and insurrection";
    - "opens the door to foreign influence and corruption, which finds a facilitated access to the government itself through the channels of party passions. Thus the policy and will of one country are subjected to the policy and will of another" (Washington, 1919, p. 22).

These accusations are not developed as arguments in the *Address*, but remain bare assertions. However, at the time of the *Address*, the United States had been in existence for eight years such that these assertions could indeed be based on some experience, rather than mere speculation as in the *Federalist Papers*.

Alexis de Tocqueville bluntly claims, "Parties are an evil inherent in free governments; but they do not have the same character and the same instincts in all periods of time" (de Tocqueville, 2012, p. 280). Yet he makes a distinction between great and small parties:

great parties "those that are attached to principles more than to their consequences, to generalities and not to particular cases, to ideas and not to men. In general, these parties have more noble traits, more generous passions, more real convictions, a more candid and bold appearance than the others" (de Tocqueville, 2012, p. 280).

small parties "are generally without political faith. Since they do not feel elevated and sustained by great objectives, their character is stamped by an egoism that occurs openly in each of their acts. They get worked up from a cold start; their language is violent, but their course is timid and uncertain. The means they use are miserable, like the very end that they propose" (de Tocqueville, 2012, pp. 280–281).

2.2. OTHER CRITICISMS OF POLITICAL PARTIES

Clearly the evils that de Tocqueville sees in political parties are those of small parties, not great parties, and his criticisms are inherent in his description of them. Additionally, he notes that "The parties that threaten the Union rest, not on principles, but on material interests" (de Tocqueville, 2012, p. 284). Moreover, he claims that the proliferation of small parties is due to the political ambitions of particular politicians, since "it is difficult to throw someone who holds power out of office for the sole reason that you want to take his place. So all the skill of politicians consists of forming parties" (de Tocqueville, 2012, p. 285).

Quagliariello notes that Louis Xavier Eyma had further developed de Tocqueville's critiques at the point that the spoils system had become established in the United States, with the effect that "Political conflict had been replaced by a war between factions that often resorted to violence and even murder. ... The fact that political life was now devoid of any nobility and had caused the 'better element' to seek refuge in the private sector had transformed public life into an area dominated by unscrupulous people who intended to further their careers and their personal finances in a shorter time than would have been possible in any other profession" (Quagliariello, 1996, p. 61). Eyma quotes an American newspaper at length, concluding with regard to the Democratic party that "Every member of this organization is subject, on pain of dismissal, to passive obedience and to the most rigorous discipline, and is inevitably transformed into an electoral broker, obliged to provide his quota of enthusiasm and to add his voice to the processions. By becoming a federal employee, he has annihilated his freedom as completely as the soldier who enlists in the army" (Eyma, 1862, p. 346).[3]

While Henry Sidgwick does not explicitly engage in a criticism of political parties and certainly does not argue for their abolition, he does consider a series of disadvantages specifically of a dual party system that would be appropriate to consider in this context. He notes that the dual party system:

- "tends to make party-spirit, if perhaps less narrow and fa-

---

[3]This quotation is my translation back from Eyma's French translation, in the absence of an alternative source for the original. Quagliariello continues to describe similar criticisms by Gustave de Molinari occasioned by the 1876 election in the United States (Quagliariello, 1996, pp. 61–63).

natical, at any rate more comprehensive and absorbing" (Sidgwick, 1891, p. 571);

- "while the two-party system diminishes in some respects the defects of parliamentary government, it intensifies them in other respects" (Sidgwick, 1891, p. 572);

- "the tendency before noted in parliamentary government of the English type, to entrust executive power to parliamentary leaders who are not specially qualified for their administrative functions, is aggravated by the permanent division into two competing parties" (Sidgwick, 1891, p. 572);

- "the dual system seems to have a dangerous tendency to degrade the profession of politics: partly from the inevitable insincerity of the relation of a party leader to the members of his own party, partly from the insincerity of his relation to the party opposed to him" (Sidgwick, 1891, p. 572).

Of course, these disadvantages have been framed with regard to a dual party system, and therefore may be remedied by adopting a different party system; yet at least some of them may indeed be indicative of fundamental problems with political parties in general.

Similarly to de Tocqueville's distinction between great and small parties, Goldwin Smith argues that whereas in revolutionary times, there was some grounds for forming parties, "But in ordinary times political opinion is not bisected any more than opinion on other subjects. Party then ceases to have any rational foundation, or to afford any moral justification for the submission of conscience to its yoke" (Smith, 1897, p. 630).[4] Therefore, he asks "whether party government after any model, British or American, is the right mark at which to aim" (Smith, 1897, p. 630). Without rational foundations, parties devolve into "self-seeking or fanatical sections" with the result that "A gang of political banditti may in this way turn a legislature into its engine" (Smith, 1897, p. 631). Consequently, Smith considers the institution of political parties to be "now apparently in a state of final disintegration. What is to come next? Representative government may be the ideal, but is it capable of being worked? That is the momentous question to

---

[4]Also discussed in (Quagliariello, 1996, pp. 123–125).

2.2. OTHER CRITICISMS OF POLITICAL PARTIES

which the next generation may be called upon to give a decisive answer" (Smith, 1897, p. 631).

One answer came from a Russian thinker based in Paris observing Great Britain and the United States. His full answer will be reviewed in Section 5.1, but his criticisms of political parties should be presented here. As noted earlier, political parties had not yet fully developed as organizations when many of the previous criticisms had been made, as they had when Moisei Ostrogorski investigated the organization of political parties in Britain (Ostrogorski, 1902a) and in America (Ostrogorski, 1902b). Based on this extensive investigation, Ostrogorski claims that political parties have faced a number of "problems confronting democratic government" (Ostrogorski, 1902b, p. 646), but have "solved [them] the wrong way, or it has increased the gradient of the incline down which these difficulties were pushing democracy" (Ostrogorski, 1902b, p. 647). Briefly, Ostrogorski claims that party formalism has:

- "repressed the individual and lowered the standard of political society";

- "deadened individual responsibility";

- "put a premium on cowardice in public life";

- "obstructed the free course of opinion, while leaving the individual defenceless against it";

- "debased the ideal";

- "degraded public morality"; and

- "reduced the citizen to a helpless instrument, which all those who exploit the public interest may manipulate as they please" (Ostrogorski, 1902b, p. 647).

Worse still, Ostrogorski thinks that these problems "have not all manifested themselves in their complete logical fulness" (Ostrogorski, 1902b, p. 647), even at the hands of American political machines.

While not uniquely responsible for these problems, political parties tend toward conformism, at least within parties, and this leads "to the enslavement of the mind" (Ostrogorski, 1902b, p. 649).

The struggle for the liberation of the mind from social and religious conventions beginning in the Enlightenment period is now threatened by the impacts of political formalism, which "adds the strength of organization. Organization gives substance to convention, brings out its latent power, intensifies it, and makes it produce the maximum of its effect" (Ostrogorski, 1902b, p. 650). The impacts of the organization of political parties ultimately lead to a vicious circle, whereby parties require even more organization the more that party organization "demoralizes the party and lowers public life" (Ostrogorski, 1902b, p. 651).

Robert Michels expands Ostrogorski's considerations into what has subsequently been termed an "Iron Law of Oligarchy" regarding political parties. Michels finds that while "The principle of organization is an absolutely essential condition for the political struggle of the masses", it is precisely their organizational factors that lead political parties to compromise democracy (Michels, 1915, p. 22). The problem is that "Organization implies the tendency toward oligarchy" (Michels, 1915, p. 32), and that as power becomes more concentrated in the hands of few leaders, their impact on the party becomes "more disastrous than in the far more extensive life of the state" (Michels, 1915, p. 33). Such concentrated power in the hands of party leaders fosters among the party members "a trust in authority which verges on the complete absence of a critical faculty" (Michels, 1915, p. 53). Consequently, leadership tends to be retained not because it is effective or needed for the challenges at hand, but simply because it is already in place (Michels, 1915, p. 98). The result is that leaders, who present themselves as servants to the cause espoused by the party, in the end become its masters (Michels, 1915, p. 154). "Thus, from a means, organization becomes an end" (Michels, 1915, p. 373), and "the party becomes a mere 'organization' " (Michels, 1915, p. 376).

Karl Mannheim notes a few dangers in the "amalgamation of politics and scientific thought" (Mannheim, 1960, p. 33) entailed by the establishment of ideology within political parties:

- Tendency toward dogmatism: "Political parties, because of the very fact of their being organized, can neither maintain an elasticity in their methods of thought nor be ready to accept any answer that might come out of their inquiries. Structurally they are public corporations and fighting orga-

2.2. OTHER CRITICISMS OF POLITICAL PARTIES 43

nizations. This in itself already forces them into a dogmatic direction. The more intellectuals became party functionaries, the more they lost the virtue of receptivity and elasticity which they had brought with them from their previous labile situation" (Mannheim, 1960, p. 34).

- Degradation of political discourse: "Political discussion possesses a character fundamentally different from academic discussion. It seeks not only to be in the right but also to demolish the basis of its opponent's social and intellectual existence. Political discussion, therefore, penetrates more profoundly into the existential foundation of thinking than the kind of discussion which thinks only in terms of a few selected 'points of view' and considers only the 'theoretical relevance' of an argument. Political conflict, since it is from the very beginning a rationalized form of the struggle for social predominance, attacks the social status of the opponent, his public prestige, and his self-confidence" (Mannheim, 1960, p. 34).

While Mannheim presents these as dangers arising specifically from the efforts of intellectuals to provide scientific arguments to justify political organizations, one might see these also as inevitable consequences of the development of political parties, regardless of the involvement of intellectuals in political parties.

Although Maurice Duverger is generally dispassionate in his analysis of political parties, he does at one point refer to "the virulence of party microbes" where in some cases "instead of using parties to ensure success at elections, elections are used to ensure the growth of parties; the party has become the end, the election the means" (Duverger, 1964, p. 367), echoing one of Weil's arguments. He also notes how political parties can help ensure that dictatorships become "a lasting regime because it is based upon a perpetually self-renewing institution, the political party" (Duverger, 1964, p. 371). Furthermore, with regard to the question of a single political party as opposed to multiple parties, Duverger notes two reasons for preferring a single party, ultimately claiming that "Really these are arguments rather for the suppression of all parties rather than the setting-up of a single party" (Duverger, 1964, pp. 261–262):

- "The first is derived largely from Rousseau and his conception of the general will, which would be falsified by being split up into collective particular wills";[5]

- "The second reason is based on considerations of fact; this pluralism is considered to be contrary to the pursuit of public good by those in power, yet this should be their supreme aim" (Duverger, 1964, p. 261).

While Duverger notes these as arguments against political parties, he does not clearly endorse any of these reasons or arguments, as will be discussed in the Conclusion.

As with Sidgwick and Duverger, Alan Ware does not explicitly engage in a criticism of political parties, but in his broader investigations of the nature of political parties, he claims that political parties in liberal democracies "have been, at most, only partly democratized themselves" (Ware, 1987, p. 216). He identifies "five aspects to this incomplete success" that are relevant here:

1. The choices presented to voters in elections may be partly obscured by parties in some electoral systems.

2. While electoral campaigning may educate citizens about political issues to some extent, campaign activities are primarily directed toward voter mobilization rather than education.

3. Political campaigns and other party objectives tend to restrict the scope of political participation by citizens.

4. Political parties tend not to emphasize democratization within their parties, and therefore this remains "an elusive objective".

5. Political parties tend to fail to find a balance between state and society, either becoming too identified with the state in

---

[5]Similarly, Quagliariello notes that "Ostrogorski was reiterating the mainstay of traditional liberalism, namely that organized groups, whether they be parties or leagues, should not set foot in government. The notion of common good would not tolerate any form of division" (Quagliariello, 1996, p. 136). However, the conception of the general will presented in Chapter 12 does seem to be compatible with this sort of division, not necessarily into political parties, but certainly into sides and factions.

some cases, or becoming too bound to interest groups "that it becomes for difficult for the parties to act as a separate force within society" (Ware, 1987, p. 216).

In reviewing these criticisms,[6] it is apparent how they shift from the external impacts of factions on states prior to the development of modern political parties in the 19th century, to the internal impacts on individuals afterward. Weil's arguments align to this shift as well, focusing on the impact of political parties on individuals, whether within the parties or outside of them. The difference between the factions criticized by early writers and the political parties criticized by later writers is the level of organization manifest in these groups, in accordance with the distinctions drawn in the Introduction. While the criticisms of factions may still apply to political parties by virtue of the opposition between different groups characteristic of both, the level of organization in political parties brings with it a new range of problems, and it is notable that later writers tend to focus on these issues arising specifically from the organizational aspect of political parties rather than reiterating the previous criticisms against factions that arguably have not been mitigated by the subsequent transformation of factions into political parties.

2.3 Additional Arguments Against Political Parties

My approach to political parties likewise aligns to this shift in focus toward the impact of political parties as organizations on individuals. In the book on technology (Ressler, 2024), I argued that organizations are products of technology and technological thinking, and that they are one key factor compromising an authentic engagement with technology. Yet organizations also impact authenticity

---

[6]See also Max Stirner's egoistic criticisms of political parties that do not translate very well outside of that egoistic context (Stirner, 1995, pp. 209–211), though some of his reflections overlap other criticisms in this chapter. Likewise, consider some blunt accusations from Nietzsche: *"What are the means by which a virtue comes to power?* By exactly the same means as a political party: slander, insinuations, undermining the opposing virtues that are already in power, changing their name, systematically persecuting and deriding them: in other words, *by means of nothing but 'immoralities'"* (Nietzsche, 2003, p. 165).

in a general way, not merely with regard to technology, so it should be expected that organizations acting in different spheres of the lives of people would thereby encourage inauthenticity in corresponding aspects among people. In particular, political parties as organizations are agents of inauthenticity in the political lives of people, in the form of political inauthenticity, as described in the Introduction.

Weil uses the metaphor of a political machine twice (Weil, 2014, pp. 11, 28), but does not develop the metaphor further. In this, I think she missed a significant opportunity. Whereas in a manufacturing setting, machinery can replace the labor of individual people, in a political setting a political party as a machine consumes people as parts of the machinery, constraining individual opinions according to the specifications and limits of what is needed to maintain the functioning of the political machine.

With regard to political machines such as Tammany Hall that were prevalent in the United States in the 19th and early 20th centuries, these organizations as such have been abolished and suppressed by subsequent laws, whereby some may think that the metaphor of a political machine does not properly apply to current political organizations such as political parties. Indeed, it is difficult to identify bosses of such political machines in the current structures of political parties, but it may simply be the case that the machinery has evolved to the point where individual bosses are no longer needed to keep the machinery in motion. I suggest that the machinery is still in place, but that it stands ready to serve whomever is in a position to activate it.

I take the following line of argument against political parties, which partially subsumes some of the previously reviewed criticisms, but focuses them specifically on the organizational impacts of political parties:

- A single political party only represents a narrow range of possible political positions.

    If there were only a single issue facing a community or a nation at any given time, then political parties might be formed to represent every possible side of the issue, thereby encompassing the full range of political positions.[7] However,

---

[7]Ostrogorski cites the experience of electoral campaigners in claiming that the

2.3. ADDITIONAL ARGUMENTS

with each additional issue that the community or nation faces, the range of possible political positions spanning all of these issues increases combinatorially. Insofar as a political party is obliged to take a position on each issue, a political party can only represent a single one of these combinations.[8] If there were just two issues, each of which had only two possible sides that could be adopted, then it is still feasible that there might be four political parties representing the full range of combinations of these sides. Yet there are typically many more issues facing an electorate at any given time, and any single issue may have more than just two possible sides that could be adopted, so the possible combinations will inevitably exceed the number of actual political parties.[9]

It may be the case that for a certain set of issues, the possible sides for one issue should be coordinated with the possible sides for another issue, in order to represent a consistent overall political stance. Yet it is not clear that such apparent consistency is necessary, but rather might itself represent a position adopted with regard to a substantive political issue at a higher level.[10] For example, suppose that one issue is whether individual citizens should be granted a particular right, and that a second issue is whether corporations should be granted that same right. Someone might claim that in the interest of consistency, those who think that individual citizens should be granted that right should likewise

---

electorate cannot comprehend more than one issue at a time (Ostrogorski, 1902b, p. 660). See Section 5.1 for a discussion of Ostrogorski's proposal based on this supposition.

[8]Although Ostrogorski notes regarding party platforms formulated at conventions: "The platform presents a long list of statements, almost on *omni re scibili et quibusdam aliis*, relating to politics, in which everybody can find something to suit him, but in which nothing is considered as of any consequence by the authors of the document, as well as by the whole convention" (Ostrogorski, 1902b, p. 261).

[9]See also (Wolff, 1970, pp. 32–34) on this point, as well as (Kedar, 2009, pp. 194–196).

[10]Sidgwick makes the following comment regarding a series of political parties formed on different issues: "There seems to be no clear general reason why any one of these parties should coincide with any other; persons convinced of the expediency of extended popular control over government might easily differ on questions relating to the limits of governmental interference, or on the proper character of the foreign policy of the State" (Sidgwick, 1891, p. 566).

hold that corporations should be granted the right as well, so that there are really only two possible positions that could properly be adopted with regard to these two issues, rather than four. Yet the demand for consistency here represents a position adopted with regard to a higher level political issue concerning whether corporations should have the same rights that individuals have, on which issue there is an opposing side. If I take the opposing side, then I may indeed judge that individuals deserve the right in question, but corporations do not, or even the reverse. Therefore an attempt to reduce the number of issues, perhaps on the part of a political party to align the electorate better to its own set of positions, may simply represent a position on a higher level issue, rather than any recognition that the full range of possible political positions is practically narrower than it logically would seem to be.[11]

John Stuart Mill discusses the importance of the freedom of expressing "standing antagonisms of practical life", giving the following examples of opinions favorable:

- "to democracy and to aristocracy"
- "to property and to equality"
- "to co-operation and to competition"
- "to luxury and to abstinence"
- "to sociality and individuality"
- "to liberty and discipline" (Mill, 1977, p. 254)

Muirhead cites this list and notes, "We could package these 'fractional truths' together (though Mill does not) into two coherent groupings, and say that liberalism and

---

[11] With regard to the dominance of two-party systems, Epstein claims, "Whether or not two-party competition is natural, or more natural than multi-party competition, the believers in its desirability want to engineer its establishment. The existence of issue-dualism is not necessary as a foundation for their position. Instead, they may seek to manufacture this dualism by creating two-party competition" (Epstein, 1967, pp. 57–58). Furthermore, "It is true that there is difficulty in finding a reasonable limit to combinations of opinions justifying separate parties. Seventy parties might be even more 'natural' than seven" (Epstein, 1967, p. 70).

conservatism form an overarching standing antagonism" (Muirhead, 2014, p. 100).[12] Indeed, these might be considered two coherent groupings, but if Muirhead is suggesting here that these are the only coherent groupings, then Muirhead owes an argument. Mill may have been inspired by the conservatism and liberalism of his era in devising his list of standing antagonisms, but it seems that many more combinations of these standing antagonisms might form coherent groupings, even if there is no ideology or political party espousing those groupings.

De Tocqueville earlier had prioritized one of these standing antagonisms specifically with regard to the United States: "I am not saying that American parties always have as their open aim, or even as their hidden aim, making aristocracy or democracy prevail in the country. I am saying that aristocratic or democratic passions are easily found at the bottom of all the parties, and, although hidden from view, they form the tender spot and the soul of the parties" (de Tocqueville, 2012, p. 286). Yet the relationship between this dichotomy and other standing antagonisms is not perfectly clear. Consider a proposed antagonism between environmentalism and industrialism that Mill does not mention. Is environmentalism aristocratic or democratic? If there is a link between these two pairs of antagonisms, it would seem that the link has changed since the era of the wealthy 19th century industrialists who could be seen as representing the aristocratic element in American society at the time. Now some may see environmentalism chiefly as the province of those who can afford to be concerned about the environment, whereas working people representing the democratic element need to support industrialism to ensure that they have jobs. Rather than attempting to link these standing antagonisms, it seems clearer simply to acknowledge that all combinations of them are possible and coherent and always were.

- Consequently, the probability that a single political party

---

[12]Though for some reason Muirhead omits sociality and individuality. Did this pair not fit neatly into the proposed dichotomy between liberalism and conservatism?

represents what is needed for a community or a nation is correspondingly small.

Suppose that for each issue facing the community or nation at any given time, there is a single side that properly represents what is optimal for that community or nation with regard to that issue at that time. Then the set of such sides across all of these issues will represent the optimal overall political position for the community or nation. Yet if a single political party can only represent a narrow range of possible political positions, as argued above, then the chance that any existing political party represents that optimal overall set of political positions diminishes as the number of issues and the number of possible sides to each issue increases.[13]

Suppose now that this prior assumption does not hold, namely that for at least some issues, there is not a single side representing what is optimal. In that case, it appears that what is needed is either a compromise or some other form of coordination between the opposing sides on the issue.[14] Yet this demand for compromise or coordination itself seems to be a possible position that might be adopted with regard to the issue and therefore already would represent a possible side to the issue that represents what is optimal for the community or nation regarding that issue, contrary to the assumption. Consequently, the point still holds.

Of course, members or adherents of political parties will claim that their party already represents that optimal set of positions, which is why they support that party. Yet members or adherents of opposing political parties will claim the same thing for their parties, equally passionately. Where political parties tend to polarize the electorate by adopting positions in direct opposition to other parties, it seems unlikely that

---

[13]This point applies not only to the entire community or nation, but also to class divisions within them. According to Michels, "The party, regarded as an entity, as a piece of mechanism, is not necessarily identifiable with the totality of its members, and still less so with the class to which these belong. ...In a party, it is far from obvious that the interests of the masses which have combined to form the party will coincide with the interests of the bureaucracy in which the party becomes personified" (Michels, 1915, p. 389).

[14]On the nature of what this other form of coordination might be, see Section 5.2 and Chapter 11.

2.3. ADDITIONAL ARGUMENTS

one set of people within a community or nation would endorse the optimal positions on all issues, where another set of people would fail to endorse an optimal position on any issue.

- Members of or adherents to a political party do not necessarily hold all of the political positions espoused by the political party naturally.

Since existing political parties represent only a narrow range of possible political positions, as argued above, the probability that a given party represents the political positions of any given citizen would appear to be as small as the probability that the positions adopted by the party represents what is needed for the community or nation as a whole. This low probability might therefore seem to extend to members or adherents of those political parties as well as citizens who are not aligned to any party. Although this conclusion does not strictly follow, nor is it necessarily the case that all party members or adherents naturally hold the positions of their respective political parties.

Someone might object that actual political parties represent clusters of positions that resonate with actual citizens, despite the purely logical possibility for alternative clusters of positions. The reason that particular political parties actually exist is that significant number of citizens agree with what those parties stand for, so the claim that the probability is low that the political party represents the political positions of its members or adherents is a faulty claim, according to this objection, once the actual probabilities are considered rather than merely the logical probabilities.

While there is some justice in this objection, it does not establish that members or adherents of political parties naturally hold all of the political positions espoused by the party.

In a section entitled "Do voters really choose?" Ware makes an important point with regard to the packages of policies offered to voters in an election: "But if voters were not ideological, then they might be faced with packages that contained some policies they wanted and some they did not. The sort of package wanted might simply not be available and, if it was not, voters could be faced with having to decide whether they felt more concerned about one issue than another" (Ware, 1987, p. 77).[15] I contend that the question of ideology is negligible in this instance, and that even voters who are ideological face such choices, since their ideology may not exactly match the ideology of any existing political party.[16]

Political scientists study the ways that voters choose among parties where there is no single party that represents the voters' preferences exactly, as noted in the quotation from Ware.[17] Voters in general tend to vote for parties that most closely match their political opinions overall, unless they vote strategically to prevent a particularly odious party or candidate from being elected. The more closely the political party's policies match a voter's preferences, the more likely the voter may be considered to be an adherent of the party. Yet such adherents do not necessarily hold all of the positions espoused by that political party, at least not initially.

Such adherents may eventually join the political party as a member, judging on balance that it is better to support the party as a member to advance the adherents' political goals, than it would be to participate in the political process merely as a voter. Although the terms of party membership may include a provision that the member must support the political party's positions, that does not mean that such members naturally hold those positions, only that they consider it better to join the party than to remain outside, even if it means accepting some positions and policies that they would not otherwise endorse.

- Political parties tend to coerce members and adherents to align themselves to positions that they do not naturally espouse.

Political parties tend to demand coherence and unanimity. If a party embodied diverse opinions among its membership,

---

[15] See also (Weinstock, 2019) and (Priest, 2014, p. 141) for similar observations.

[16] See Chapter 10 on the irrelevance of ideology to the abolition of political parties.

[17] See (Downs, 1957), (Dalton & Wattenberg, 2000), (Dalton & Klingemann, 2009), and (Kedar, 2009).

particularly if that diversity becomes internally contentious, then voters may see the party as weak and in disarray and may therefore be disinclined to vote for that party. Consequently, political parties will tend to align everyone associated with the party toward the canonical positions and policies adopted by the party in the cause of party unity, to ensure that voters perceive it as a strong party and vote for it.

This pressure toward unity and uniformity increases the more closely that one aligns oneself to a party. With regard to voters in general, disagreement with party policies may indeed be tolerated by that political party, so long as the party ultimately gets the voters' votes.[18] With regard to voters who are adherents of the party, who may be in a position to influence other voters, more unity is demanded, to ensure that voters in general are not getting mixed messages with regard to the party's positions and policies. With regard to members of a political party, absolute unity and uniformity is demanded, and may indeed be a condition of membership in the party.

This aspect of the functioning of political parties was documented extensively in Ostrogorski's study, such as the tactics used by political parties to ensure that discordant voices are not heard in committees (Ostrogorski, 1902b, pp. 213 ff). Indeed, such coercion ultimately succeeds best when it becomes second nature to party members, such that it does not even occur to them that the party's positions or policies may be challenged: "I know it's true, it comes from the national committee" (Ostrogorski, 1902b, p. 329). Nor does there seem to be evidence that this aspect of political parties has changed significantly since Ostrogorski wrote.

However, Duverger argues that public opinion is to a significant extend the consequence of party systems in any case. "Parties tend to crystallize opinion; they give skeletal articulation to a shapeless and jelly-like mass" (Duverger, 1964, p. 378). Against those who criticize the distorting effects of political parties on public opinion, he replies that "it is in-

---

[18] Epstein states a point that he considers to be obvious: "The party may act as though it has a mandate for all its policies, but it is well understood that not all of its voters really preferred the party's stand on every policy" (Epstein, 1967, p. 268).

evitable and really is much less deformation than formation. They fail to realize that raw opinion is elusive, that formed opinion alone can be expressed, and that the method of expression necessarily imposes on it a frame which modifies it" (Duverger, 1964, p. 380). More bluntly he claims, "In fact raw opinion does not exist, at least it is not ascertainable" (Duverger, 1964, p. 382).

One might agree with Duverger with regard to the illusion of raw opinion, but challenge the superiority of political parties in forming public opinion with regard to political matters.[19] Political parties have an interest in obtaining and maintaining power and in fostering the growth of their parties, as Weil has argued, and therefore will seek to form public opinion in terms that are favorable to their interests, not necessarily to the public interest, though each of them will claim that those interests are the same.[20] Consequently, political parties are not the best frame to impose on unformed public opinion, as Duverger expresses it. Yet political parties will impose their frames and will seek to align members, adherents, and voters to the positions adopted by each political party within that frame.

- As organizations, political parties align and reduce people to specific roles.

  Organizations imply organized structures of relationships, where members of the organizations are assigned roles within those structures, roles that enable certain functions to accomplish the organization's goals, but that also limit the ways in which individual people can function within the organization.

  Those in leadership roles have predefined functions that they are expected to perform to keep the party machinery functioning. Candidates for office are expected to campaign for those offices, then to serve in those offices to enact party

---

[19] See also (Neumann, 1956, pp. 396–397), (Poguntke, 1996, p. 320), and (Farrell & Webb, 2000, p. 124).

[20] For example: "the established parties in a party system may be seen to have a mutual interest in the survival of their particular conflict and their particular form of competition" (Mair, 1997, p. 14). See also (Sartori, 2005, p. 45).

2.3. ADDITIONAL ARGUMENTS

policies. Members in general are fundamentally in the role of sources of funding and of guaranteed votes. Even outside the party organization, people tend to be reduced to roles, whether as political opponents or merely as voters. These roles tend to circumscribe the ways that political parties interact with people. For example, in the case of voters, so long as the voter casts a vote in favor of the political party, it does not matter much what the voter actually thinks, whether the voter agrees with all of the party's policies, or none at all. Nor does it matter whether the political party's policies actually benefit those voters or not. Accountability to voters is only vaguely associated with the threat that a voter might not cast a vote in the party's favor in the next election, but until that election, the party may ignore the voter entirely, unless there is a threat that voters may recall an elected member of the party. The role of voters is merely to cast a vote, preferably in favor of a political party.[21]

These roles are accentuated when other organizations become affiliated with the political party. For example, a media outlet such as a newspaper or a television network may become an agent for party publicity or even for blatant propaganda. A think tank may become the primary means for developing party positions and policies. These roles and functions may become so dispersed among other organizations that the political party itself becomes merely a central linking node in a network of organizations without any real power in itself, with the consequence that it would seem that no one is really in charge of the political party.

- The roles in political parties that seek to persuade voters are different from the roles that set the positions and policies that voters are to be persuaded to endorse or at least to enable with their votes.

Suppose that there were a political party that consisted of a single individual. Then that person would be required to

---

[21]Duverger analyzes the roles within a mass party, starting with a distinction between supporters and members (Duverger, 1964, pp. 62 ff), and proposing the following hierarchy: "the militants lead the members, the members lead the supporters, the supporters lead the electors" (Duverger, 1964, p. 114).

fulfill all of the roles needed by the political party to function, including the formation of positions and policies that the party will espouse, campaigning for office as the party's candidate, as well as the publicity of those positions and the persuasion of voters to vote for the party's candidate. In the process of campaigning, the candidate would typically confront individual voters in attempting to seek their votes, and in the course of this interaction, may be persuaded by voters to adopt different policies in order to serve the voters' interests. In this case, forming policy, campaigning for office, and persuading voters will all align, since these functions and roles are all served by a single individual. Of course, in this case, the idea of a political party is vacuous, since the single individual functions essentially as an independent candidate for office.

In an actual political party, these roles are served by different individuals, and in some cases, by different organizations, as noted above. Those in roles that are in contact with voters who might be persuaded by them to reconsider the party's policies are different from those in roles that formulate and endorse those policies. Consequently, the party structure isolates the mechanism of persuasion from the possibility of being persuaded.

For example, in the case of a party member serving in a role attempting to persuade prospective voters, perhaps by going door to door to elicit support for the party and its candidates, that party member might encounter a particularly persuasive voter with a compelling argument against one of the political party's policies. Yet even if that party member is personally convinced that the party's policy is flawed, that member has little chance of changing the party's policies or of convincing any of the party's candidates for office to go against the party's policies, specifically by virtue of the restrictions accorded to that member's role.

Even in the case of a candidate for office, if that candidate encounters a persuasive voter with a compelling argument and is personally persuaded not to endorse the party's policy, it is unlikely that this one candidate will be able to change the party's positions and policies, or even to stop the party's publicity functions from publicizing that policy. More likely, the party would pressure the candidate to fall in line with the party's positions and policies, or to risk getting ejected from the party, with the resulting withdrawal of funding from the candidate's campaign, as well as the full impact of the party's publicity function undermining the candidate's credibility and character.

There are certainly exceptions to this pattern, however. For example, a candidate for a particularly high office, such as President or Prime Minister, has much more influence over the direction and policies of a political party than a candidate for a minor local office. Additionally, if a particularly persuasive voter with a compelling argument against a policy happens to be extremely wealthy and threatens to withhold donations to the party, that argument would be financially persuasive in addition to whatever logical or rational force it may have on its own. Yet in general, the structure of a political party makes these exceptions rare and unlikely for any individual voter to have influence over the positions and policies of the party, regardless of how compelling an argument the voter may have.

- Therefore, political parties are machines for persuasion that cannot themselves be persuaded, but that push for positions and policies that do not clearly represent the natural opinions of its members or the best interests of the community or nation.

This conclusion does not mean that political parties can never be influenced. Indeed they can, particularly at key moments, such as in a primary election in which the direction of the party in the full election will be determined. However, this influence does not constitute persuasion, by means of rational argument, for example, but rather takes the form of broader social and economic forces acting in aggregate, as well as the contrary influences of what other political parties are doing at the time.

The machinery in question is precisely the organizational structure of the party relegating people to the status of roles. These roles tend to limit the scope of what individual people do in a political context, such that the operation of a political party becomes relatively uncomplicated by the full range of values and goals inherent in complete individual people, leaving the organizational structure to operate smoothly in pursuit of whatever narrow range of possible positions the political party happens to endorse at the time.

Ostrogorski is particularly sensitive to the metaphor of political parties as machines throughout his study, at one point quoting Joseph Cowen who attempted to run for a seat in Parliament counter to the Liberal Party Caucus at the time, saying "What the Caucus wants is a political machine. I am a man, not a machine" (Ostrogorski, 1902a, p. 240). Shortly afterward, Ostrogorski quotes Undersecretary of State Leonard Courtney saying, "I think we see in our country a tendency of machinery to supersede individuality, and a tendency on the part of the people to trust to machinery instead of maintaining individual activity" (Ostrogorski, 1902a, p. 241), leading to the establishment by means of the Caucus system in Great Britain "a government by machine instead of a responsible government by human beings" (Ostrogorski, 1902a, p. 595). In the United States, this metaphor had become so potent that Ostrogorki devotes two entire chapters to "The Politicians and the Machine" (Ostrogorski, 1902b, pp. 367–440).

The resulting machinery encourages political inauthenticity, as described in the Introduction, namely an automatic alignment to the values, decisions, and actions of a political party or other similar organizations, rather than any critical assessment of these values, decisions, and actions individually. Since political parties do not clearly represent all of the positions and policies that citizens naturally hold, even as members of those parties, the political inauthenticity they foster primarily serves to further the goals of the political parties themselves, not the citizens, regardless of what role those citizens serve with regard to political parties, with the possible exception of a few ambitious individuals who are able to seize the mechanism of political parties to serve their own interests..

Thus the arguments from Weil and others do not exhaust the possible arguments against political parties, as evidenced by this

2.3. ADDITIONAL ARGUMENTS

further line of argument, and it seems likely that as political parties evolve and adapt to changing political conditions, the grounds for possible argumentation against political parties expand accordingly. The line of argumentation in this section will likely not be the last word against political parties either. In every instantiation and incarnation, political parties have proved themselves to be problematic, and these problems appear to be cumulative. The arguments raised by Bolingbroke against the political parties of his time, which I characterize as factions according to the distinctions in the Introduction, can still be raised against modern political parties, for example, and likewise with the arguments from other writers against the political parties of their time. This suggests something fundamentally faulty with political parties that cannot be eradicated, but that rather tends to accumulate additional problems, however much political parties may develop over time. My line of argumentation in this section attempts to uncover what is fundamentally flawed with political parties, but even this argument may not completely have identified the root problems with political parties, as may become clear if political parties are allowed to persist and to evolve.

Weil claims that political parties are "an almost unmixed evil" (Weil, 2014, p. 28), and the accumulation of arguments against them seem to support the assessment of that evil. However, that conclusion would be premature at this point, since only the negative arguments have been considered. What needs to be considered as well is whether the alleged evils of political parties are mixed with benefits that come uniquely from political parties, which requires an investigation into the functions that political parties serve, to which the next chapter will be devoted.

Chapter 3

Realignment of Functions of Political Parties

Suppose that the arguments outlined against political parties in the previous chapter succeed, as I believe that they do, and that political parties are acknowledged to be problematic organizations, compromising the political freedoms of people. The activities of political parties that result in the adverse affects reviewed in those arguments are not the only activities that a political party may perform, and if some of these activities serve necessary functions within a democracy, then it seems that political parties cannot simply be abolished, as Weil recommends. The key question to ask is for whom are those functions performed? For the benefit of the political party and its candidates only? Or do the functions also serve the broader democratic society? Perhaps Hume's attitude toward the political parties of his day is still valid, and that political parties must be tolerated as a necessary evil.

Alternatively, perhaps those functions themselves are indeed necessary within a democracy, but they could be performed by some other means, perhaps better than political parties do, without the adverse effects resulting from political parties. In that case, if those necessary functions can be realigned to other groups or institutions besides political parties, then the argument against political parties would be complete. Perhaps not only are political parties responsible for adverse effects within a democracy, but any positive function they serve could be served without political parties, assuming that these functions need to be performed at all.

Anthony King summarizes six such functions of political parties, which "seem to be the main ones referred to in the literature":

1. the structuring of the vote;

2. the integration and mobilization of the mass public;

3. the recruitment of political leaders;

4. the organization of government;

5. the formation of public policy; and

6. the aggregation of interests (King, 1969, p. 120)

This chapter will review these functions to determine whether these functions need to be served within a democracy, and if they do, whether they can be served in other ways without relying on political parties.[1]

3.1 The Structuring of the Vote

"All that is meant by the awkward word 'structuring' is the imposition of an order or pattern enabling voters to choose candidates according to their labels (whether or not the labels appear on the ballot)" (Epstein, 1967, p. 77). As King notes, "a group or organization that did not attempt to structure the vote in its own favor would not normally be called a party" (King, 1969, p. 120). Immediately, it seems that invoking the function of structuring the vote as a reason to retain political parties would simply beg the question. Why does a healthy democracy need to have candidates for office associated with party labels at all, particularly if those labels are designed to favor political parties themselves?

Rather, this function seems to be part of the problem with political parties, that they tend to use labels to influence voter behavior rather than the quality of the candidates that they offer for office. If I consider myself a good party member, then why should I expend any amount of time evaluating the candidates

---

[1] For other lists of the functions of political parties, see for example (LaPalombara & Weiner, 1966, p. 3), (Kirchheimer, 1966, p. 188–189), (Nanetti, 1988, p. 172), and (Dalton & Wattenberg, 2000, p. 5). I believe that these lists may largely be subsumed under King's list.

3.1. THE STRUCTURING OF THE VOTE

for any political office, so long as I can simply choose whatever candidate bears the label of my party? After all, if the party has endorsed the candidate for the office, then the candidate must also be a good party member, and the party must believe that the candidate would serve well in the office, so I need not waste any amount of time considering who should get my vote for that office. If I did perform an evaluation of candidates, then I would likely just end up choosing the same candidate that the party endorsed. In fact, I might end up thinking that I actually have a duty to vote for the party's candidate, simply by virtue of my membership in the party, even if I have evidence that the candidate is not worthy of my vote at all, perhaps even evidence of serious misconduct on the candidate's part.[2]

Yet it would be hasty to reject this function by focusing too closely on party labels as a means for structuring the vote. The reason that party labels may be valuable on a ballot is that they help voters decide how to vote, even if voters do not slavishly vote for all candidates that bear a particular party's label. If I am faced with a long list of candidates for an office, possibly on a ballot with a long list of offices to elect, it may not be clear exactly how I want to cast a vote for every office. Candidates for high profile offices who have been featured in the media may have made an impression on me, such that it is clear how I intend to vote for those offices, but candidates for lower level offices may not even have come to my attention. Even if I researched every office on the ballot, evaluated every candidate, and made my voting choices in advance of coming to the polling place, I may not remember every candidate's name when I come to complete my ballot, assuming that I did not write my preferences on a piece of paper that I brought with me. Party labels may help me recall the voting preferences that I had previously established. For example, I may recall that for Office 1, I liked the candidate for Party A, but for Office 2, the candidate for Party B impressed me, whereas for Office 3, I preferred the independent candidate whose name started with the letter 'R'.

Indeed, one may wish that every voter would have researched all of the candidates in advance of casting votes, but practically speaking such a wish would be in vain. Not every voter will have

---

[2]Indeed, even if political parties do not strictly have members, those who associate themselves with a party simply by registering to vote under that party label often consider it a duty to vote for whatever candidate the party nominates.

the time or the inclination to perform an adequate evaluation of all candidates before the election, and in some cases, voters may not have access to the resources needed to conduct such an evaluation. Consequently, voters may in the end simply be influenced by whatever advertising or propaganda has reached them about particular candidates. Yet if this is the case, it should also be challenged whether party labels constitute an adequate means for structuring the vote for such voters, since their perception of political parties themselves will likely have been influenced by advertising and propaganda as well. Perhaps I had researched political parties in the past, comparing their principles and policies in order to decide how to align myself politically, but those parties may have shifted in recent years, such that my personal political values are now best served by a different political party, or perhaps by no political party at all.

If the function of structuring the vote is to help voters choose candidates that align with their political values, rather than to help political parties influence voters in their favor, then other means of structuring the vote could be considered. For example, if one accepts a political spectrum from left to right, from liberal to conservative,[3] then the vote might be structured simply across this spectrum, possibly offering more finely grained structuring than mere party labels could provide, depending on the number of political parties that are active in any given voting district. So if the spectrum is scaled between 0 and 10, where 0 is the most liberal, 5 is moderate, and 10 is the most conservative, then the vote could be structured numerically across this spectrum. The ballot itself might even include such numerical assessments next to the candidates' names, or perhaps even a color gradient based on such a numerical assessment.

Assignments of such numerical structuring might occur in different ways. Political parties might indeed make such assignments themselves, thereby providing additional distinctions within a political range in which a party considers itself to function. In offices

---

[3] Note that I personally do not accept such a political spectrum, and I refuse to allow my political orientation to be plotted on a line from left to right. That quite literally constitutes one-dimensional thinking, and I think constructive political discourse and governance is compromised when such a spectrum is imposed. As soon as one places oneself on some partisan spectrum, however abstract, one has already fallen into a political error.

3.1. THE STRUCTURING OF THE VOTE 65

for which political parties may nominate multiple candidates from the same party, the numerical assignment across the political spectrum may be different for different candidates that the party nominates, thereby possibly offering some inducement for moderate voters to vote for at least one of that party's candidates, for example.

Yet political parties are not critical for such an assessment, since candidates themselves could assign their own position on such a political spectrum without any party influence. It might be part of the process to register to appear on the ballot for the candidate to submit what position on the spectrum the candidate would like shown on the ballot. Of course, a given candidate may misrepresent that candidate's actual position on the spectrum in order to influence voters, but function in office according a different position on the spectrum, if elected.

In order to provide a more objective assessment, perhaps an independent institution might run a series of questionnaires for all candidates and evaluate each candidate's position on the spectrum according to some publicly available criterion. That institution could be a governmental agency or a non-profit, non-partisan private organization, depending on the relevant community's level of trust with the objectivity of government agencies or private organizations.

Yet it would be better to have a more detailed assessment over multiple dimensions, rather than simply providing voters with a single position for each candidate on a political spectrum. For example, such an assessment might be conducted across the range of relevant issues at the time, even if the one-dimensional political spectrum is still accepted for each issue. Perhaps a voter may be interested in a more conservative candidate with regard to one issue, but a more liberal candidate with regard to another. Assuming that candidates are not all one-dimensional and that each candidate is not assessed at the same position along the political spectrum for all issues, a voter would thereby be given more information whereby to decide how to vote. Of course, such a multi-dimensional assessment would be difficult to present on a ballot, so perhaps the ballot might show a single aggregate assessment for the candidate, while the more detailed assessment is made available to voters prior to the election.

The preceding proposal is only one way to structure the vote without relying on party labels. There may be others. Arguably the proposal for structuring offered here provides a better guide for voters than party labels, and the proposal does not require political parties. In fact, political parties may compromise such structuring by attempting to manipulate assessments in their favor by misrepresenting the assessments their candidates to align them to current political trends in order to get them elected.

In any case, whether the function of structuring the vote is essential to democracy or not, it is not a function that requires political parties.

3.2 The Integration and Mobilization of the Mass Public

As King explains, integration and mobilization refer "to the processes whereby individuals acquire psychological and social attachments to political parties and, through them, to the wider political order" (King, 1969, p. 124). Here again, if the question is why political parties must be part of the wider political order, then invoking this function would clearly beg the question.

Insofar as such integration and mobilization involves "psychological and social attachments to political parties" this function likewise seems to represent a problem with political parties, where political parties tend to rely on such psychological and social attachments to attract members and voters rather than a rational assessment of the party's positions and proposals. If I am a member of a particular political party mainly because all my friends, family, and associates are members of that political party, then the choice of that political party would seem not to be an authentic choice. I am merely following the relevant groups to which I belong. This does not mean that one cannot make an authentic choice to be a member of the same party that one's friends, family, and associates happen to belong to,[4] but political parties tend to encourage such inauthentic choices precisely by seeking to integrate and to mobilize more members of the public into their parties.

---

[4] See (Ressler, 2024, Chapter 5).

3.2. INTEGRATION AND MOBILIZATION

However, in an attempt to interpret this function more broadly, integration here might be understood as integration with the constitutional political system in which voters participate. By seeking to involve potential voters, political parties are incorporating them within the broader political process. In other words, political parties serve a function of inculcating civics in the broader population.

Yet it is not clear that political parties are the best means for performing this function. A public education system seems better suited to teaching civics to young members of the community, since it is more likely to do so in an objective fashion than under partisan influences, unless of course that educational system has specifically been constrained by those partisan influences. Political parties will tend primarily to serve their own interests, even in ostensibly serving a public function. They will not be inclined to emphasize aspects of the political process from which they will not benefit, or indeed which benefit their political opponents more than benefits them.

Additionally, mobilization might charitably be interpreted as increasing direct participation in the political process by encouraging members of the community to vote. This function is typically called "getting out the vote" and indeed may seem to be an important function that needs to be served in a healthy democracy. If citizens in a democracy increasingly fail to vote, whether due to dislike of the candidates who are offered to them or even due to apathy with regard to the entire process, then the electoral power of those who do vote increases accordingly. If only a small minority of eligible voters actually vote, then the alleged democracy may functionally become more like an oligarchy.

Yet here again it is not clear that political parties are the best means to perform this function either. Political parties certainly encourage potential voters to participate who are likely to support them, but they do not tend to encourage voters who are likely to support their political opponents. Historically, political parties have been instrumental in actively attempting to prevent supporters of their opponents from voting, whether through direct means such as threatening violence or through indirect means such as imposing poll taxes.

However, if each political party is actively encouraging its own voting base and discouraging its opponents' voting bases, then it might be thought that the dynamics of this pattern of voter influence would balance out, so long as electoral laws provide equal opportunities for all political parties by prohibiting violence, poll taxes, and other fundamentally problematic practices. If my own political party is encouraging me to vote, and the opponents of my political party are encouraging me not to vote, then I will clearly listen to my own political party and disregard the others, and similarly for members or adherents of other political parties, such that the competing attempts to influence voters would be canceled out. However, this apparent balance does not account for the attempts to influence independent voters and countenances legal though undemocratic influences to persuade some voters to participate and others not to participate.

If there is a goal to encourage broad or even universal participation in the voting process for eligible voters, then a more effective means for achieving this goal would be to make voting mandatory, as in Belgium and Australia at the time of writing, for example. Rather than trusting voter mobilization to competing interests of political parties or even trusting in the civic spirit of voters to participate, a committed democracy might enact laws to ensure that voters perform their electoral duties.

For my part, though, I am not sure that mandatory voting is desirable within a democracy, and in fact seems somewhat undemocratic. The right to vote is indeed a right, but most rights entail the right not to exercise that right. If I actively choose not to vote, then that choice represents my political decision at the time. It effectively counts as a null vote. If I lived in a community that did enact mandatory voting, and I wanted to vote for some offices but not for others, then I would want to ensure that each office included an option whereby I could actively indicate my null vote, such as an option indicating "None of the above". If however I were compelled to vote for some candidate, when I actively reject all candidates on a ballot, that compulsion hardly seems democratic.

It might be objected that these considerations could apply to voters who actively and intentionally choose not to vote, but not to prospective voters who are merely apathetic about voting in general. To the contrary, I consider such apathy likewise to constitute a null vote just as much as an active choice not to vote. If a potential voter is not sufficiently motivated even to consider the question of whether to vote or not, then that apathy reflects the political situation in the relevant community, regarding the quality of candidates for office, as well as the system of political parties, the electoral system, and even the form of government. If most people in a community are apathetic about voting, leaving the electoral choices to a small minority, then it would seem that the community does not really want a democracy after all.[5]

Consequently, I argue that this alleged function of integration and mobilization does not need to be served at all, and if it does need to be served, it is not best served by political parties.

3.3 The Recruitment of Political Leaders

In a healthy democracy, the recruitment of potential political leaders is indeed an important function that needs to be served not only in some way, but in a manner that is conducive to democratic practices. If candidates for office were recruited only by the incumbent of that office, namely if each incumbent selected the successor to that office, to the exclusion of all other potential candidates, then the resulting political system could hardly be understood as a democracy. Yet if no candidates for offices of political leadership were recruited at all, thereby leaving ballots empty, then it would not merely be the case that democracy was not being practiced, it would represent a breakdown of the constitutional government, requiring the imposition of some other means for selecting leadership besides elections to ensure that the government does not simply collapse for lack of anyone to lead it.

However, this latter case seems highly improbable. For the highest elected offices, there does not seem to be any lack of people interested in serving within those offices, manifest in particular by the presence of independent candidates outside of any party membership or affiliation who actively seek such offices.

Lester G. Seligman identifies four mechanisms for selection of candidates *within* a political party:

Self-recruitment "wherein the individual is the initial and primary instigator of his candidacy";

---

[5]For a stronger position on the subject of mandatory voting, see Jason Brennan's arguments in (Brennan, 2012; Brennan & Hill, 2014; Brennan, 2017). While sympathetic to Brennan's line of argument, I am not committed to his stronger positions concerning the possibility of duties *not* to vote.

Sponsorship "makes the candidate the agent of interest groups and organizations";

Conscription "In this type a candidate is drafted to run for office or is appointed to political posts and accepts the discipline of the group that chooses him"; and

Co-Optation "invites and enlists established political influence into party leadership in order to strengthen party organization and/or mass support" (Seligman, 1967, pp. 312–313).

While conscription and co-optation seem primarily restricted to the functioning of a political party,[6] self-recruitment and sponsorship are not, so these mechanisms could be used to recruit candidates for offices in the absence of political parties. Of course, sponsorship would be employed by some interest group or other political organization, so even if the organization is not a political party, there may be concerns about the influence of such groups and organizations on the political process. However, the arguments in this study are focused specifically on political parties, and it seems clear that there are mechanisms to recruit candidates for office available that do not rely on political parties, or indeed any organization at all, which is the point of the discussion here.

Yet with regard to lower offices at the local or municipal level, the case is not so clear. Political parties tend to seek candidates for all such offices to ensure that their party policies are implemented at all levels of government. If a particular political office is not competitive in a certain election, given the nature of the electorate or the very high level of popularity of a competing political party's candidate, a political party may decide not to run a candidate for that office, in order to save campaign funds for more competitive races. However, in general, a political party tends to recruit candidates for all available offices within its area of influence, whether national, regional, or local, to demonstrate to voters that it is a significant party within that area. If a political party only ran a few

---

[6]Although one might imagine a candidate conscripted by the incumbent of an office, not affiliated with a political party, seeking to establish a successor who would continue the policies of the incumbent. This possibility would not compromise the argument here, though it would pose problems for democratic practice in general if this were the only mechanism employed, as suggested above.

3.3. THE RECRUITMENT OF POLITICAL LEADERS

candidates, that may signal to voters that the party itself is weak and lacks influence, even if the particular candidates that the party nominates are strong.

In such lower offices, it may happen that self-recruitment fails in the absence of political parties, if no one eligible for those offices is sufficiently motivated to run for office. Furthermore, the office may not be sufficiently important or influential for an interest group or other political organization besides a political party to sponsor any candidate. Political parties themselves can provide motivation for potential candidates who are conscripted for such offices in the form of inducement toward advancement within the party or toward higher offices, as described in (Seligman, 1967, pp. 304–306). If an individual serves well in a relatively unimportant lower office, then that effective service could induce the political party to support the individual's candidacy for increasingly higher offices. In this way, the ambition of potential political candidates enables political parties to find individuals who may be conscripted to stand for office at even lower levels of government.

It is possible for ambition to function the same way in self-recruitment in the absence political parties, namely that individuals recognize that in order to become a viable candidate for higher office, they will need to prove themselves politically competent in lower offices. However, it is not clear that such ambition will enable the self-recruitment of candidates for every office at every level of government, without the influence of political parties.

It is not clear how strong the risk may be for lower offices to fail to secure any candidates whatsoever within a particular election in the absence of political parties; however, this risk is not sufficiently great in itself to support an argument for the necessity of political parties to serve the function of recruiting political leaders. Even if it could be established that there is a very high risk that ballots for some lower offices may be devoid of any candidate for some election, there are alternatives for filling such offices. For example, if no candidate appears on a ballot, the relevant constitution may specify that the head of the next highest jurisdiction will simply appoint someone to serve within that office, essentially formalizing a process of conscription within the constitution. For example, if no candidate stands for the office of mayor for a town, the governor of the region in which the town is located might appoint that mayor, thereby enabling that level of government to continue functioning.

While not democratically optimal, this situation is not necessarily undemocratic either. Where this constitutional provision is widely known, the political stakes in the election of the head of the next highest jurisdiction become accordingly higher, such that members of each community within that jurisdiction may feel more motivated to vote for the head of that jurisdiction in each election, to ensure that the possible appointment of leadership within lower offices would be performed better than would happen on election of some alternative.

In any case, even though the recruitment of leaders is an important function that needs to be served within a democracy, there are alternatives to the influence of political parties in fulfilling this function.[7]

3.4 The Organization of Government

There are systems of government whereby the right to organize the government is constitutionally granted to the party that secures a majority of seats in the legislature, or that organizes a coalition encompassing a majority of seats, as in the Westminster system of government. In these cases, however, what is at stake with regard to political parties is not fundamentally whether the function of the organization of government can be performed independently of political parties, but whether the value that political parties provide the communities under such constitutions outweigh the problems that political parties foster, as argued in Chapter 2, or whether those constitutions should be amended to eliminate the influence of political parties altogether. The following discussion, though, will focus on systems of government in which political parties are not granted an explicit role by the constitution.

King notes that the function of organization of government is often not clearly defined in the literature on political parties, suggesting that "What is meant is the arrangements under which, or the processes whereby, persons in government or the various elements of government come to act in concert" (King, 1969, p. 132). He proceeds to question the extend to which political parties actually serve this function, particularly in the United States (King,

---

[7] See Section 4.2 for additional considerations of this function specifically with regard to the conduct of elections without political parties.

1969, p. 134). Since "the organization of government may be achieved constitutionally, extra-constitutionally, formally or informally" (King, 1969, p. 132), it seems immediately clear that such organization of government does not necessarily depend upon political parties, particularly if organization of government is achieved constitutionally or formally in ways in which political parties are not granted an explicit role.

Furthermore, it is not clear that political parties provide the best means for organizing government. When they do organize government, political parties tend to organize it to maximize the influence of the party within that government, within the limits imposed by the relevant constitution. The resulting governmental organization along party lines does not necessarily serve the needs of everyone subject to the government, certainly not for those who oppose the political party that imposes the particular organization on government. One might rather demand that government is always organized in a way that best serves the people who are governed, regardless of which political party elects the lead executive or the majority of the members of the legislature, even if the policies that are enacted by the government are strongly influenced by political parties. Yet political parties tend primarily to follow their own interests in organizing governments when given the opportunity, to maximize their power.

Consequently, the function of the organization of government is neither necessarily nor best served by political parties.

3.5 The Formation of Public Policy

In questioning the extent to which political parties form public policy, King lists three ways in which political parties can exert influence of public policy:

1. "by influencing the content of political thought and discussion;"

2. "by adopting specific policies or programs which the party's leaders, once elected, feel constrained (for whatever reason) to implement;" or

3. "by successfully bringing pressure to bear on government, as when a governing party's followers in the legislature or

in the country use the processes of the party to force the government to adopt particular policies" (King, 1969, p. 136).

Yet immediately King claims "that organized parties in the United States do not play a central role in forming public policy and probably never have" (King, 1969, p. 136), and further "Nor have party organizations outside the United States been particularly successful in imposing their will when their own leaders have either formed the government or participated in a governing coalition" (King, 1969, p. 137). Consequently, insofar as public policy is already being formed without the strong influence of political parties, this is not a function that necessarily requires political parties.

The arguments in Chapter 2 likewise indicate that political parties are not the best agents to entrust with the formation of public policy, at least if the interests of the members of the public are considered paramount as opposed to the interests of political parties. Weil argues that the ultimate goal of political parties is their own unlimited growth, in which case the interests of the public are not the most important goal of political parties, despite what they may claim. Furthermore, if my arguments are correct that political parties do not completely represent the political positions even of members or adherents of those parties, but rather tend to coerce people into aligning themselves with the positions adopted by political parties, then the resulting public policies formed by political parties will not necessarily represent the interests even of the members or adherents of those parties.

Consequently, the formation of public policy is neither necessarily nor best entrusted to political parties either.

3.6 The Aggregation of Interests

King notes that the aggregation of interests "overlaps all of the functions discussed already" (King, 1969, p. 137), since apparently one must aggregate the interests of members or adherents of a political party in order to maintain a sufficiently strong organization capable of performing those other functions. Yet the overlap of the previous functions immediately suggests that if those functions do not require political parties, then the aggregation of interests is not a function that necessitates political parties either.

3.6. THE AGGREGATION OF INTERESTS

Indeed, King claims "In a diffuse way interest aggregation of one sort or another undoubtedly takes place in all political systems just as it takes place in all societies, associations, interest groups, trade unions, bowling clubs, and families" (King, 1969, p. 139). To the question "Are parties in fact the major interest aggregators in the West?" King simply replies "no" (King, 1969, p. 139).

This alleged function of political parties has puzzled me since I first heard the term 'aggregation of interests'. What puzzled me was why this function was associated with political parties at all. The place where aggregation of interests ought to occur should be at the level of the relevant community as a whole, not any sub-group or faction within that community. Any aggregation of interests at the level of a political party leaves the aggregation of interests in the community as a whole unresolved, and in fact compromises it by concentrating interests within the bounds of a few parties, resulting in polarization within the community according to the structure of the political parties.

The way that political parties tend to aggregate interests merely reiterates the criticism of political parties in Chapter 2. The tendency of political parties is not to mediate among the opinions of its members to develop a position that represents a coordination or even a compromise between them. Rather, a political party tends to start with a position on some issue, then to gather members and adherents around it. Where the party is obliged to take a position on other issues, likely in response to its opponents, it tends to adopt the position reactively, then to align its members or adherents to that position. Thus, the pattern of aggregation in an aggregation of interests within a political party is mainly to oblige its members or adherents to adopt the position that the party takes, asserting pressure in various forms to achieve alignment on positions, whether merely by suggesting that those who take a contrary position are not "good party members" or by threatening to expel dissidents from the party.

This aggregation pattern is similar to the pattern of leveling that Kierkegaard notes in the abstraction of *the public* that features in the question of authenticity,[8] but whereas the leveling of *the public* tends to stifle anything exceptional in people above the average level of mediocrity in the group, the aggregation of inter-

---

[8] See (Kierkegaard, 1978, p. 84) and the discussion in (Ressler, 2024, pp. 86 ff).

ests in a political party tends to stifle dissent not against the average political positions in the community as a whole, but rather against the positions that the political parties have taken or have been obliged to adopt in order to differentiate themselves from their political opponents. Yet the result is similar, in that members of the political party are herded into a narrow range of political opinions, just as members of *the public* are herded into a narrow range of mediocrity.

If the aggregation of interests is more properly directed toward the community as a whole, then this aggregation should be a function of a legislature or similar institutions, not political parties. At their best, such institutions seek to build consensus around policies that incorporate the interests of all within the community. At their worst, they become arenas for political contests whereby one faction seeks to defeat the interests of other factions in order to make one set of interests prevail and to increase the power of the faction. Political parties tends to encourage the latter.

In any case, the aggregation of interests cannot be a function that necessitates the existence of political parties.

3.7 The Support of Partisan Ideals

Since King compiled his list of six functions of political parties, a number of authors have defended political parties somewhat obliquely, by distinguishing partisanship from support for political parties, arguing for the virtues of partisanship, then arguing that political parties have the function of supporting those partisan virtues.[9]

Throughout the course of this book, partisanship has been understood precisely as support for political parties, where no distinction is made between being anti-partisan and anti-party. While the full meaning of the word 'partisan' supports such a distinction, whereby one may be a partisan to a cause without necessarily supporting any political party, the common linguistic roots and con-

---

[9] Most notably, (Rosenblum, 2010), (Muirhead, 2014), and (White & Ypi, 2016), though Muirhead does not insist on a distinction between partisanship and support for political parties, but rather acknowledges as I do that partisanship "refers to the political orientation of citizens who *stand with a party*" (Muirhead, 2006, p. 714), (Muirhead, 2014, p. x). See also (White & Ypi, 2010), (White & Ypi, 2011), (Muirhead & Rosenblum, 2012), (Muirhead, 2019), and (White & Ypi, 2019).

3.7. THE SUPPORT OF PARTISAN IDEALS

temporary usage of these terms make sustaining such a distinction highly strained, particularly if one wants to make a broader public argument outside of academic contexts. For the same reasons, attempting to maintain a distinction between partisanship and support for political parties may encourage equivocation on the part either of the reader or even of the author, where in any argument regarding either partisanship or political parties it may be challenged whether the argument stands on its own logical merits or whether it is supported mainly by an illicit conflation between terms.[10]

The distinctions in Table 1.1 in the Introduction are intended to capture the essence of any proposed distinction between being partisan and supporting a political party without risking equivocation. One may take a side on an issue without thereby supporting a political party, even a political party that strongly champions the same side of that issue. The key factor, as presented in Table 1.1, is the relationship to organizations, where taking a side on an issue in itself has no necessary relationship to organizations, whereas political parties are understood precisely as organizations.

Yet my distinction regarding taking sides as opposed to supporting political parties does not capture everything that champions of partisanship claim in their defense of the notion. Partisanship for them is "advocacy on behalf of groups and causes" (Rosenblum, 2010, p. 60), a political identity (Rosenblum, 2010, p. 342), or standing "in a certain relation to other who share similar views" (White & Ypi, 2016, p. 5).[11] Merely taking a side is not active enough to qualify as partisanship to its defenders, where the difference precisely constitutes the virtues of partisanship for them. It is one thing to hold an opinion on an issue, but quite another to

---

[10] For example, Rosenblum's section entitled "Preliminary Articles in Defense of Partisanship" (Rosenblum, 2010, pp. 356 ff) appeals to party identification and partisans of political parties to support the alleged virtues of inclusiveness, comprehensiveness, and disposition to compromise, during which it is not clear whether the distinction between partisanship and adherence to political parties is strictly being honored and whether political parties are supporting the argument for partisanship or the reverse.

[11] As indicated in a previous footnote, for Muirhead, partisanship "refers to the political orientation of citizens who *stand with a party*" (Muirhead, 2006, p. 714), consistent with my usage of the term in this book. Consequently, partisanship does not mean exactly the same thing to each of its defenders, but they are agreed that it is vital for democracy.

have the conviction and commitment to do something about it.[12]

For my purposes, though, the notions in Table 1.1 were not intended to capture any virtues associated with them, but merely to make a set of principled distinctions between kinds of groups that did not make any value judgements among them, as is clearly evidenced among those who attempted to distinguish political parties from factions before the development of modern political parties.[13] Indeed, among those who take a side on an issue, there are those who believe so strongly in the issue that they are motivated to take action in order to ensure that the resolution of that issue that they support is enacted, but some do not. Yet the same is true for factions, caucuses, and even political parties. Just because one is aligned to one of these groups does not necessarily indicate that one is particularly motivated to take any significant action. One might align to a political party and identify with it, but not bother even to vote, let alone to engage in any campaign activity in support of the party. Consequently, I think it is important to separate the distinctions between kinds of groups from any distinctions concerning the degree of commitment to such groups. In order to evaluate the arguments of the contemporary champions of partisanship, however, the distinction between partisanship and support of political parties will provisionally be accepted.

After warning against assuming "that partisanship itself is a defense of parties" (Rosenblum, 2010, p. 4), Rosenblum mounts precisely such a defense, claiming to "flip the common-sense view that partisans support parties" (Rosenblum, 2010, p. 367), "arguing that parties are necessary to realize the value of partisanship" (Rosenblum, 2010, p. 457). Such an argument posits a function that

---

[12](Rosenblum, 2010, pp. 354–356).

[13]As do many of the contemporary champions of partisanship as well, such as (Muirhead, 2006, pp. 32–36) and (White & Ypi, 2016, pp. 32–54). Rosenblum does not seem to put much stock in the distinction between factions and parties, though she cites many who do. Interestingly, Goodin remarks regarding early texts distinguishing between factions and parties that they "were all written with aims more political than philosophical. The political world that they addressed was only a very partially democratized one. There are limits to what such history can teach us" (Goodin, 2008, p. 208). Here I agree with Goodin, at least until he continues to remark on the irony "that, were we trying to imagine what a No-Party Democracy might be like, we can do no better than to try to imagine ourselves into the ideal political world of the American Founders themselves" (Goodin, 2008, p. 208). Goodin's subsequent imaginative attempts will be strongly criticized later in this section.

3.7. THE SUPPORT OF PARTISAN IDEALS

political parties appear to serve within the context of this chapter, namely to realize the value of partisanship. Since partisanship is a political virtue, and political parties are necessary to realize this virtue, then the abolition of political parties would therefore compromise this political virtue, according to this line of argument.

One might challenge this argument on various grounds. One might question whether partisanship is actually a virtue as it is claimed. Rosenblum argues that "partisanship rather than voting simply is a significant underpinning of democratic participation and stability" (Rosenblum, 2010, p. 356).[14] With regard to stability, this is not the stability of a government or a nation, but rather what "allows parties to carry on in the long run, despite political vicissitudes and electoral defeats" (Rosenblum, 2010, p. 355). I would count this kind of stability a conditional virtue at best. If the political movement itself has value, then such stability would indeed have as much value as the political movement itself. However, if the movement is discriminatory, oppressive, or adverse to other political virtues, then the value of the stability that sustains it would be correspondingly negative.[15]

With regard to participation, I am willing to accept it as a political virtue, but I challenge the extent and degree to which this virtue must be manifest across the entire citizenry. Voting, which Rosenblum contrasts with partisanship in the passage cited above, does indeed count as political participation, despite Rosenblum's insinuations that this level of participation is insufficient. Yet if every citizen increased political participation to the level that would satisfy Rosenblum's conception of partisanship, then it would seem that some of what those citizens are currently doing would not be accomplished, including other important social activities, given the limitations on the time available to each citizen, and it is not clear that one could claim on democratic principles that all citizens must exhibit political participation to that degree, rather than merely asking citizens periodically to vote and preferably to vote in an informed manner. In that case, the degree of participation inherent in Rosenblum's conception of partisanship must apply only to a subset of the citizenry, though how much and in what degree is still uncertain. Still, like the recruitment of political leaders, a func-

---

[14] Presumably Rosenblum here means "partisanship rather than *simply* voting".

[15] See also the considerations in Chapter 15.

tion of a political party need not apply to every citizen in order to count as an important function within a democracy.

More importantly for the purposes of this chapter, one might challenge whether political parties are strictly necessary to realize the value of partisanship. Indeed, one might propose a facile counter-argument concerning the kind of partisanship that leads to the creation of new political parties. Are political parties necessary for that partisanship? If so, then how would political parties ever start in the first place? Yet I think the challenge here must be stronger. I have noticed that most invocations of necessity in arguments within political science fail to satisfy the logical requirements to establish necessity, in which case I tend to interpret such references to necessity rather loosely and charitably, in the sense of being historically very important rather than being strictly necessary. Rosenblum has certainly not established strict necessity in her claims regarding political parties and partisanship. If there are alternatives to political parties in their proposed function of realizing the alleged virtues inherent in partisanship, then those alternatives may indeed be better than political parties, given the problems with political parties catalogued in the previous chapter and more extensively in Rosenblum's own book, and given that the other functions of political parties likewise have alternatives, as discussed in earlier sections in this chapter. Consequently, the challenge is simply that the case for the necessity of political parties to realize the value of partisanship has not been made, even though it may be accepted that they have been historically important to it.

Before evaluating a different argument linking political parties and partisanship that does attempt to make this case, I note another ground for challenging the argument concerning this alleged function of political parties.[16] Champions of partisanship are careful to clarify that they are not defending all forms of partisanship, typically making distinctions between good and bad partisanship.[17] Consequently, partisanship in these arguments is not

---

[16] See also the questions raised against Rosenblum's critique of independence in (Bader & Bonotti, 2014).

[17] Rosenblum claims that "What is needed is not more independence but more and better partisanship" (Rosenblum, 2010, p. 368), which implies that there is worse partisanship, which she herself catalogs in the bulk of her book. Muirhead distinguishes between high and low partisanship (Muirhead, 2014, pp. xii,

3.7. THE SUPPORT OF PARTISAN IDEALS

defended in all of its forms, but only in an ideal form.[18] Of course, an appeal to an ideal here is not problematic in itself. If political parties could make the difference between the achievement of the highest ideals of partisanship and the further degradation of partisanship, then the argument would seem to have some merit. However, it is not political parties as currently constituted that serve this role, but political parties that themselves meet some ideal conditions.[19] Consequently, the argument suffers from what might be called a *problem of compounded ideals*. For one ideal to depend upon the achievement of another ideal puts the former ideal at considerable risk. For the purposes of this chapter, this problem tends to undermine completely the argument under consideration, since if political parties did exemplify their ideals, then the problems identified in Chapter 2 presumably would not occur and recur, in which case there would be no need to investigate and to evaluate the functions of political parties in determining whether they ought to be abolished or merely amended, and therefore partisanship would not be raised as an issue, whether ideal or actual.

Consider a different argument for the function of political parties, offered by White and Ypi. They identify a function that they claim political parties serve, namely preserving "the vitality of the democratic ethos itself, understood as a positive conviction amongst citizens of the worth of engaging with collective political agency so as to exercise the fundamental democratic principle of collective self-rule" (White & Ypi, 2010, p. 809), ultimately analyzed into three factors. Consistent with the purposes of this chapter, they consider with regard to these factors whether "under contemporary conditions there are other actors which may perform them equally well or better" than political parties (White & Ypi, 2010, p. 817).

The argument proceeds by first identifying three factors key to this alleged function:

---

202). White and Ypi separate partisanship's empirical and normative dimensions (White & Ypi, 2016, p. 9). Zelizer distinguishes responsible partisanship from hyperpartisanship (Zelizer, 2025).

[18]White and Ypi explicitly concede that "the reality of partisanship often fails to live up to this ideal" (White & Ypi, 2016, p. 54).

[19]White and Ypi are particularly assiduous in making such a clarification: "Perhaps no existing political group fits the model precisely" (White & Ypi, 2016, p. 25).

	normative	motivational	executive
social movements	yes	yes	no
corporate actors	no	yes	yes
deliberative fora	yes	no	possibly

Table 3.1: Summary of White and Ypi's evaluation regarding sources of conviction provided by alternatives to political parties

> ...at least since the advent of democracy as collective self-rule, conviction in the worth of collective political agency has drawn on three sources: first, an ability amongst citizens to articulate political ideals that can be addressed through collective action (the *normative* source); second, a willingness to see these goals as ours, in the sense that our own fate or that of those with whom we identify is bound up in their achievement, and that they may require 'our' collective engagement to be met (the *motivational* source); and third an understanding that political agency can be institutionally applied to secure them (the *executive* source). (White & Ypi, 2010, pp. 809-810)

After arguing that political parties indeed provide these sources for the conviction of the worth of collective political agency, they proceed to consider three alternatives that might provide these sources in place of political parties, namely social movements, corporate actors, and deliberative fora, then to evaluate the extent to which each of them might provide these sources. The results of their evaluation are indicated in Table 3.1, summarized from (White & Ypi, 2010, p. 821).

White and Ypi therefore conclude "If conviction in the worth of political agency derives from three main sources — normative, motivational and executive — it seems that parties offer a contribution that none of the other familiar actors in contemporary politics can match" (White & Ypi, 2010, p. 821).

Here again, there are multiple ways to challenge this argument. One might challenge whether the alleged function of political parties is actually served by political parties, as White and Ypi claim. Certainly, they do argue explicitly that political parties provide the three sources of conviction, and they further argue against claims that political parties are incapable of providing these three functions (White & Ypi, 2010, p. 817–821). However, they admit "that the three roles identified for parties in this article are currently weakly performed" (White & Ypi, 2010, p. 821). Thus, it seems the problem of compounded ideals might be raised here. Despite this admission, though, I think that one can accept that political parties do serve this function, though not very well.

Alternatively, one might question whether this function is actually required. Accordingly, one might challenge the following points:

1. Whether "the vitality of the democratic ethos" is properly "understood as a positive conviction amongst citizens of the worth of engaging with collective political agency so as to exercise the fundamental democratic principle of collective self-rule" (White & Ypi, 2010, p. 809).

2. Whether this positive conviction does actually have its source in the three factors that White and Ypi identify.

Rather than pursue either of these options, I will merely note that it would be strange if every other function of political parties either is not strictly needed or could be served by other means, but that political parties are ultimately required in order to provide a positive conviction of the value of collective political action.

I think the greatest challenge to White's and Ypi's argument, however, concerns the question whether this function can be served by other means, particularly since it is explicitly part of their argument that political parties play a unique role in serving this function. Firstly, White and Ypi evaluate three alternatives to political parties, but these are only "familiar actors in contemporary politics" (White & Ypi, 2010, p. 821). They do not and cannot claim that these are the only three alternatives to political parties. It may be that there are other alternatives besides these three that White and Ypi have overlooked, or even that new alternatives may be developed that have not yet been conceived. I myself do not have an alternative to propose here, but I think there is an even stronger challenge to this aspect of White's and Ypi's argument.

Secondly, in their evaluation of the alternatives to political parties, White and Ypi conclude that none of the three alternatives can provide all three sources of positive conviction, namely normative, motivational, and executive, but that political parties can. Why should this matter? As seen in Table 3.1, while no single alternative can provide all three sources, all three alternatives together cover all three sources, with some sources covered by multiple alternatives. Even if one accepts White's and Ypi's arguments that these three sources of positive conviction are necessary for "the vitality of the democratic ethos", they have not argued that these three sources must be provided by a single actor, and it is not clear what that argument could be. It seems reasonable to insist that the three sources must be coordinated among each other, in particular that the motivational and executive sources are directed to the same policies that are dictated by the normative sources, which could easily be achieved if the same actor provides all three sources. However, it certainly seems possible for the three alternatives that White and Ypi evaluate to coordinate among each other to provide these sources and therefore to serve the democratic function in question in the absence of political parties.

Nor is it clear that it is best for a single actor to provide all three of these sources. Indeed, one might argue that part of the problem with political parties is precisely that they seek to provide all three sources from within a single organization. If these sources were distributed across multiple organizations, the effort to coordinate and to align these sources may result in a more compelling set of policies presented to voters than what comes out of a single organization seeking to align everyone to a party line. White and Ypi would need to provide an argument that such coordination between multiple actors is not possible or that any such coordination would be worse for democracy than what political parties provide. Yet since they acknowledge that political parties are currently only poorly providing these three sources for conviction of the value of collective political action, it is not clear how they can make such an argument.

Consequently, I conclude that the argument from White and Ypi cannot be used for the purposes of this chapter to show that political parties uniquely serve some vital function such that their abolition would compromise democracy. Not only has the argument failed to evaluate all possible alternatives to political parties, but the argument relies on a dubious presupposition that a single political actor must provide all of the sources for the conviction of the value of collective political action.

3.7. THE SUPPORT OF PARTISAN IDEALS

Rosenblum as well as White and Ypi approvingly cite an argument from Goodin in support of their own arguments. In an otherwise well-argued book, Goodin engages in a thought experiment imagining "what it would be like to have a No-Party Democracy" (Goodin, 2008, p. 205). The following explicit argument appears as a consequence:

1. Democracy requires that a community is collectively self-legislating.
2. A *ratio* is required to have truly 'given a law to yourself', and to be 'self-legislating' in that sense.
3. A collective *ratio* is necessarily absent from the uncoordinated votes of independent actors in a No-Party Democracy.

From the combination of these three propositions, it follows that

4. No-Party Democracy is not democracy at all. (Goodin, 2008, pp. 213–214)

The key to diagnosing the problem with this argument is understanding what Goodin means by a *ratio*. According to Goodin's initial explanation, it is a "rationale, or grounds behind the law" (Goodin, 2008, p. 213). This is required in a democracy, because

> we — citizens, as much as judges — need to know the underlying *ratio* in order to interpret and apply the law as we attempt to 'follow' it. On other analyses, the law's *ratio* might be thought to provide a rationale to legitimize the law substantively. On the present analysis, the need for the law to have a single, coherent, *ratio* derives simply from what is involved in rule-following at all. (Goodin, 2008, p. 213)

Under this interpretation of *ratio*, the faulty premise in Goodin's argument is clearly premise (3). Just because independent actors are voting in an uncoordinated manner does not mean that that there is no *ratio*, and since Goodin claims that this necessarily follows from his supposition of a No-Party Democracy, premise (3) is not merely false, but represents a logical fallacy. It does not follow from the definition of a No-Party Democracy, unless Goodin explicitly defines it as such, and if he does define it that way, such a definition would amount to begging the question. If the premise does not follow from a definition, then it represents the fallacy of overlooking alternatives concerning how a No-Party Democracy would work. Suppose in a No-Party Democracy that I am a legislator, and I propose legislation, providing an extensive rationale for why the legislation should be adopted, drafting the legislation such that it provides sufficient grounds for interpretation, and arguing why the legislation is better than any other available alternative. My fellow legislators debate the proposed legislation, and a majority votes to adopt it, all without the influence of any political party, in accordance with the supposition of a No-Party Democracy. Clearly this scenario deliberately provides a "rationale, or grounds behind the law" as Goodin requires, contrary to premise (3) of his argument. Why does Goodin overlook this alternative?

One possibility lies in a later explication of a *ratio*:

> *Democracy* requires that the *ratio* be provided by a programme that has been endorsed by the citizens. That speaks to the issue of what it is to 'give laws to *ourselves*'. A Patriot King can provide decrees with a *ratio*. Only a party that has been duly elected can provide a *ratio* that satisfies that further requirement of *democratic* rule. (Goodin, 2008, p. 217)

This presentation adds the notion of a *programme* that was not present in the earlier explication. If by a *programme* Goodin simply means a "rationale, or grounds behind the law" as he has said before, then it is not clear that only a political party can provide such a *programme*. Suppose in my earlier example, that I had campaigned for office on the strength of my proposal for the legislation in question, providing the rationale for adopting the legislation as part of my campaign speeches. Suppose further that other legislators campaign precisely on the promise of supporting my proposed legislation. If we are all elected to office, and the legislation is adopted, then the alleged requirement for a *ratio* provided by a *programme* would thereby be fulfilled.

Just because votes in a No-Party Democracy are not coordinated by political parties does not mean that they cannot be coordinated at all. I might indeed coordinate my electoral campaign

3.7. THE SUPPORT OF PARTISAN IDEALS

with the campaigns of other candidates who are on the same side of a particular issue as I am, to ensure that we have sufficient representation within the legislature to enact the legislation that we believe is needed. None of this entails that we have thereby formed a political party, just that we are coordinating political action to achieve a goal. This seems to count as partisanship according to contemporary champions of partisanship, but without the establishment of an organization, there can be no political party, according to both their distinctions and mine.[20]

If by a *programme* Goodin means an overarching ideology under which candidates campaign, then it is simply false that a No-Party Democracy necessarily entails that such a *programme* as ideology is absent. It is perfectly plausible for a candidate for office to espouse a particular ideology without being part of a political party that adopts that ideology, for example, for a candidate to campaign as a Libertarian in a nation without a Libertarian party. Under this interpretation of *programme*, not only would premise (3) be false, but so would premise (2), since self-legislation does not require an overarching ideology, at least not without further argument on Goodin's part, so this interpretation cannot represent what Goodin means by a *programme*.

On the other hand, if by *programme* Goodin means a platform of policies that a political party has adopted prior to an election, then he is clearly begging the question against those who would advocate a No-Party Democracy. Yes, without political parties, there necessarily cannot be party platforms. However, this would beg the question by requiring a party platform as a *ratio* in premise (2) as a condition of being self-legislating. I would like thereby to conclude that this interpretation cannot represent what Goodin means by a *programme*, but I suspect that it is precisely what he means, else there would be no reason to introduce the term 'programme' in addition to his earlier characterization of a *ratio* as a rationale.

Further, it does not even seem that political parties can properly provide the *ratio* that Goodin seeks here in terms of a *programme* either. As noted in Section 2.3, voters cast votes for parties according to how closely a party matches their political views compared to other parties, even if voters do not completely agree with

---

[20] On the issue of organizing without organizations, see Chapter 15.

all of the policies offered to voters in the party platforms or *programmes*. Consequently, when enacting legislation on these policies, a political party elected to power cannot assume that it has a mandate from voters on every policy in their platform, since it possible that a majority of voters who cast votes for that political party in fact oppose a particular policy, though they think that the political party would do a better job of governing than any of its rival parties on other issues. In that case, the policy in question might have a *ratio*, but it would not have been endorsed by the citizens, in which case it would seem not to be a case of democratic rule according to Goodin. Unless an election is conducted on the basis on one and only one issue,[21] it may be unclear which policies that form part of a political party's *programme* actually have been endorsed by means of the election.

Consequently, Goodin seems to rely on some fallacy whatever interpretation is given to his conception of a *programme*. These fallacies seem to be enabled by Goodin hiding behind the Latin term *ratio*, which encourages equivocation on this term, another fallacy, rather than stating his meaning in clear English and applying it consistently.

Besides the problems with the interpretation and application of the term *ratio*, one might challenge Goodin's argument on the grounds of what it means to be self-legislating. One might accept the requirement to be self-legislating in premise (1), and indeed accept the need for a *ratio* in premise (2) in terms of a rationale in accordance with Goodin's argument concerning following rules. Yet for Goodin to claim further that this *ratio* must "be provided by a programme that has been endorsed by the citizens" (Goodin, 2008, 217) suggests an interpretation of democratic representation according to which the representative is a delegate elected by citizens to honor campaign promises to support certain policies, rather than an interpretation of a representative as a trustee entrusted by the electorate to make decisions on their behalf,[22] else if legislators act as trustees and enact legislation that citizens have not endorsed, then presumably Goodin would consider that legislation to lack a *ratio* and thereby fail to meet his standards of demo-

---

[21] As Ostrogorski proposed, which will be discussed in Section 5.1.

[22] The distinction as presented is from (Farrell, 2001, pp. 170–171), but (Pitkin, 1967) investigates many more possible interpretations of representation. These distinctions will be important in the discussion in Section 5.2.

3.7. THE SUPPORT OF PARTISAN IDEALS

cratic rule. Yet since this interpretation of representation can be contested, as evidenced by the difference in interpretations noted here, then premises (1) and (2) of Goodin's argument can likewise be challenged if they presuppose a particular interpretation of representation.

I devote a significant amount of time in criticizing this argument from Goodin because I consider it to be representative of a large number of arguments against the abolition of political parties, most of which ultimately either beg the question against antipartisanship or overlook alternatives for what a democracy without political parties would entail, possibly aided by equivocation on some key term.[23] I cannot claim to have reviewed all such arguments, but I am willing to wager based on the arguments that I have reviewed that they rely on some faulty presupposition or even logical fallacy. With regard to the other arguments reviewed earlier holding that political parties serve a key function in supporting partisan ideals, none of them can be maintained for the purposes of this chapter, and I think further that the problems identified with them undermine the purposes for which the authors introduce them.

This chapter has investigated six functions attributed to political parties that are commonly mentioned in the literature on political parties, as well as a new alleged function in support of partisanship. For each of these functions, either the function could be served by some means other than by political parties, and typically better served than by parties, or the function does not strictly need to be served within a democracy, because the function primarily serves the political parties themselves, not the broader democratic community. Other functions might be identified, but I expect that they can likewise be dismissed with comparable arguments.

While Chapter 2 argued that political parties are fundamentally problematic organizations, this chapter confirmed that there is no necessary function that only political parties serve such that they should be considered necessary evils, as Hume held, for example.

---

[23] As noted earlier, the remainder of Goodin's book seems well-argued, but once the topic of political parties and their possible abolition is raised, the logical fallacies suddenly appear. I am tempted to think that this is not merely coincidental. There is something about political parties that brings out the worst in people, even in political scientists.

Consequently, I concur with Weil's recommendation that political parties should be abolished.

Chapter 4

Elections without Political Parties

The previous chapter completed the negative argument against political parties begun in Chapter 2, but it also raised some practical questions concerning how a modern democracy might operate in the absence of political parties, should they be abolished as recommended. In Section 3.4, it was noted that the Westminster system of government grants the right to form a government to the party that holds the majority of seats in Parliament or that leads a coalition representing a majority of seats. If political parties are abolished in nations adopting the Westminster system, then constitutional changes would appear to be necessary in order for governments to form. Changes to constitutions for nations not adopting the Westminster system might not be needed, for example, in the United States, whose constitution does not even mention political parties.

Additional questions were raised or suggested in the previous chapter concerning the conduct of elections and the practice of government in the absence of political parties. This chapter therefore begins the positive argument concerning how these aspects of politics and government might proceed without political parties, continued in the next chapter. This positive argument will inevitably be incomplete, since it is nearly impossible to know in advance the full range of possibilities for political structures and institutions under different social and political conditions, particularly having been under the adverse influence of political parties for so long.

The focus of this chapter will be elections, including the conduct of elections under different electoral systems in the absence of political parties. While some electoral systems may simply need to be abandoned, since they depend fundamentally upon political parties, others may need to be adjusted in order to ensure that they function optimally without political parties.

4.1 Electoral Systems

The impact of the abolition of political parties will depend upon the electoral system operative in the nation, region, or community. To understand these impacts, I follow David M. Farrell's categorization of electoral systems described in (Farrell, 2001), ignoring some of the complications that Farrell explores.

Consider the following forms of electoral systems:

Single Member Plurality System For each office on the ballot, a single representative will be chosen to represent a single district. The candidate whose receives more votes than any of the other candidates will be elected to the office. (Farrell, 2001, pp. 19–48)

Majoritarian Systems Similarly to the Single Member Plurality System, a single representative is elected for a district; however, the candidate who is elected must receive a majority of all votes cast, not just a plurality compared to the other candidates. Since it is highly possible that no candidate will receive a majority of votes in the first round of voting, particularly if there are many candidates standing for office, such systems incorporate some mechanism for eliminating candidates based on the first round of voting until a single candidate gains the majority of votes.

One mechanism is a second round of voting, where candidates performing poorly in the first round of voting are eliminated, whether by eliminating candidates who fail to meet a certain threshold of votes or by simply taking the top two candidates into the second round.

Another mechanism is to conduct a single round of voting, but to require voters to rank candidates in order of prefer-

4.1. ELECTORAL SYSTEMS

ence. If a candidate fails to gain a majority of first preference votes in the first vote count, the candidate who gains the fewest first preference votes is eliminated and the votes cast as first preferences for that candidate are allocated to the candidates who are indicated as those voters' second preferences. The process is repeated until a single candidate gains a majority of votes. (Farrell, 2001, pp.49–67)

List Systems of Proportional Representation
Eligible political parties create a list of candidates that they propose for office. Based on how voters cast their votes for these lists or candidates, representatives are allocated from the lists of candidates according to the proportion of votes cast for the political parties. There is considerable variation in such systems according to whether voters are able to vote for individual candidates within party lists or whether they must vote for a list as a whole, what minimum quota may be required for parties to be allocated any seats, and which formula is used to allocate seats proportionally. (Farrell, 2001, pp. 68–96)

Single Transferrable Vote Voting districts elect multiple candidates, and a quota is established employing some formula according to which all candidates who receive sufficient votes to meet that quota are elected to office. Voters are required to rank candidates in order of preference. After the first round of vote counting, candidates who meet the quota based on primary preferences are considered elected, and the surplus votes in excess of the quota are allocated to the remaining candidates according to the second preferences of the voters. Subsequent rounds of vote counting are performed until no surplus votes can be transferred to other candidates, possibly also by transferring votes from the candidates with the lowest number of votes, with some provision for how to allocate any remaining seats that cannot be claimed by any candidate by these means. (Farrell, 2001, pp. 121–152)

Mixed Systems Several of the systems described above are used for the same set of offices within the same level of government, typically by allocating a certain number of seats within the legislature to members chosen individually and another number of seats to be chosen according to political party. Voters may either cast separate votes for these separate classes of seats, or voters may cast a single vote that will be used both to determine representatives elected individually and to allocate seats proportionally by political party. (Farrell, 2001, pp. 97–120)

As suggested in this very brief summary of the general kinds of electoral systems, there are many variations of these systems, including the procedures for allocating votes, as well as the formulas for computing quotas. What is most relevant to this discussion is the part that political parties play within these systems, so the particular procedures and formulas that complicate these systems will be ignored.

Since Proportional Representation is proportional across political parties, if political parties are abolished, then clearly this electoral system will no longer be feasible. Likewise, Mixed Systems could no longer incorporate elements of Proportional Representation either, though they might combine elements of the remaining systems.

Proportional Representation is often advocated precisely because of its proportionality, and adherents claim that this provides the best overall method for representing the electorate as a whole. However, if political parties are problematic and do not actually represent the interests of their adherents very well, as argued in Chapter 2, then proportioning representation across political parties does not provide the desired representation of the electorate after all.

Michael Dummett notes a dilemma for voters, related to the dual purpose that Dummett claims for a general election, namely to decide (1) "who is to represent each individual constituency in Parliament"; and (2) "what the overall composition of Parliament by political party is to be" (Dummett, 1997, p. 2). Consequently, voters may be in a dilemma if they favor a particular political party and wish to see that party dominant in Parliament, but they dislike the particular person that the party has offered as a candidate for their local constituency. However, this is only a dilemma if the voters favor some political party. If voters accept the negative arguments in Chapters 2 and 3 that political parties are problematic

4.1. ELECTORAL SYSTEMS

and that their functions can be distributed to other institutions, if they need to be performed at all, then the dilemma vanishes. The concern over the composition of the legislature by political parties is replaced by a concern whether the legislature should be dominated by political parties at all, which is partly determined by the voter's choice of the representative in the local constituency. Note that Dummett considers political parties to be "an inescapable evil" (Dummett, 1997, p. 32), as does Hume. By contrast, this study has argued that the evil of political parties is not necessary at all, and it seeks to understand how elections might best proceed without them.

Some consider Single Transferrable Vote also to provide a measure of proportionality in its electoral system, but it does not rely fundamentally on political parties. However, Farrell notes that there are problems evaluating its level of proportionality, partly due to its focus on candidates rather than political parties, which would have provided an easier means for assessing its degree of proportionality (Farrell, 2001, p. 155). If political parties were abolished, then perhaps some political scientists would therefore not consider Single Transferrable Vote to provide proportionality at all, if proportionality continues to be understood as proportionality according to party. To the contrary, I would argue that proportionality could still be recognized, but it would constitute a level of proportionality among the political tendencies of particular candidates, perhaps aligned to a scale ranging from most liberal to most conservative, as suggested in Section 3.1. This proportionality would thereby represent how liberal or conservative the resulting legislature should be, where individual voter preferences might best be indicated by a mix of candidates within the constituency rather than the political tendencies of just one political party or just one candidate that happens to appear on the ballot.

Yet the kind of proportionality that Single Transferrable Vote provides seems to be primarily a function of its multi-member constituencies, and secondarily a function of its preference voting, rather than a function of the transferability of votes, the latter of which appears to be responsible for the features that lead Dummett to call it "a quasi-chaotic system" (Dummett, 1997, p. 149).[1]

---

[1] Dummett argues in favor of adopting a better system than Single Transferrable Vote, ultimately suggesting one that he calls the "Quota/Borda System"

Consequently, there appears to be opportunities to achieve this form of proportionality in other electoral systems such as Plurality or Majoritarian systems by introducing multi-member constituencies into such systems.[2]

For Plurality systems, some measure of proportionality might be implemented by granting voters as many votes as there are seats to be filled in a multi-member constituency, where the candidates getting the largest number of votes are assigned available seats until all seats are filled. If voters were granted only a single vote in such a case, the multi-member constituencies would fail to achieve any additional measure of proportionality than in Single Member Plurality Systems, since only each voter's primary choice would be reflected in the resulting distribution of seats in the legislature.

For Majoritarian systems, the incorporation of a multi-member constituency would require a different understanding of what a majority would mean in this case. If a majority is understood in terms of the majority of all votes cast, then only one member could be elected in any multi-member constituency, thus defeating the purpose of introducing multi-member constituencies. Instead, a majority might be understood in terms of the majority of voters casting votes. By granting voters as many votes as there are seats to be filled, it is thereby possible for multiple candidates to receive votes from a majority of voters. Elections in which fewer than the number of seats are allocated by candidates gaining votes from a majority of voters might be resolved by a second round of voting or by implementing ranked choice voting, as in Single Member Majoritarian Systems.

However, this interpretation of a majority in a multi-member constituency could result in more candidates gaining votes from a majority of voters than there are seats to be filled. Suppose that there are three candidates for a constituency with two seats. There are thus three combinations of two candidates that voters could select in order to allocate their two votes. If an equal number of voters choose each of the three combinations, then each candidate will have received the same number of total votes, equal to two-

---

(Dummett, 1997, p. 154).

[2] This strategy for proportionality is favored in (Dummett, 1997, pp. 121–137), though Dummett primarily considers this feature to be implemented in terms of quotas, resulting in his proposal for a "Quota/Borda System", as cited above.

thirds of the number of voters. In this case, all three candidates will have received votes from a majority of voters, but only two of them can be allocated seats, leaving the election apparently undecided.

Of course, a similar situation may occur in Single Member Majoritarian Systems, if there are only two candidates who gain an equal number of votes in the first round of voting. Consequently, whatever means are devised to resolve such indeterminacies in Single Member Majoritarian Systems could be adopted in Multi-Member Majoritarian Systems, whether they are resolved by a run-off election, by a vote from a relevant legislature, or by appointment by a relevant governor, president, or prime minister.

However, these complications are considered here only on the assumption that greater proportionality was desired by means of the introduction of multi-member constituencies. Without this addition, both Single Member Plurality Systems or Majoritarian Systems could still function without political parties.

What has become known as Duverger's law, though, seems to raise questions about these systems. Duverger offers the following proposition: "*the simple-majority single-ballot system favors the two-party system*" (Duverger, 1964, p. 217), based on an empirical correlation between such systems. This proposition would raise concerns about the employment of such a system in a democracy without political parties, if indeed it might tend toward the re-introduction of political parties in the form of a two-party system.

Yet as described by Farrell, at least, neither the Single Member Plurality System nor Majoritarian Systems necessarily fall under Duverger's law. Single Member Plurality Systems are not simple majority systems, since they merely demand a plurality of votes, not a majority of votes. Majoritarian Systems indeed demand a majority of votes, but these are not necessarily *simple* majorities or single ballot systems. Farrell describes two methods whereby the failure of any candidate to achieve a majority of votes are resolved, namely (1) two-round systems whereby only the top candidates from the first round are included in the second round of voting, and (2) alternative vote, sometimes characterized as an instant run-off, whereby voters rank candidates in order of preference, and if no candidate gains a majority of first-preference votes, the bottom candidates are progressively eliminated and the second preferences of voters for those candidates are distributed to other candidates. It should be clear, then, that Duverger's law does not apply in any of these cases.

In reflecting on Duverger's law, though, it seems to me that a simple majority, single ballot system favors not only a two-party system, but a party system in general, given the difficulty in securing a majority of voters for any particular candidate if the competitive field is too large, without a second ballot. In such cases, it would seem almost necessary to create strong organizations that could gather sufficient support around a single candidate to gain a majority of votes, and once one such organization appears, opponents will inevitably form other such organizations to combat it, ultimately stabilizing around two major organizations as Duverger proposes. So perhaps the adoption of this form of electoral system in early modern democracies should also be counted as one of the factors encouraging the rise of political parties in such democracies,[3] confirming a suspicion that a democracy seeking freedom from political parties should avoid such an electoral system if it wishes to ensure that political parties do not re-emerge in the future.

In any case, the abolition of political parties would still leave several available electoral systems that would be compatible with the absence of political parties, with opportunities for some measure of proportionality, if such proportionality were desired in some form other than proportionality by political party.

---

[3] For example, the election of the President in the United States seems to exemplify the kind of electoral system Duverger considers, since it depends on a simple majority of votes from the Electoral College, whose composition is determined by a popular vote, and there is no second vote either by the Electoral College or by the broader electorate if no candidate gains a majority of votes from the Electoral College. In such a case, the President is elected by the House of Representatives from among the five candidates gaining the highest number of votes. Indeed, this electoral system does seem to have encouraged the development of political parties in the United States. Consequently, if the United States abolishes political parties, then a constitutional amendment should modify the electoral system for this office. Of course, since the Electoral College was introduced in the constitution to implement a compromise based on conditions that no longer exist in the United States, such a constitutional amendment can be motivated even if political parties are not abolished.

4.2 Recruitment of Candidates

The best electoral system, if there is one, would still serve the aims of democracy poorly if the only candidates for office were poor ones, nominated primarily to serve the interests of political parties rather than the interests of the broader society. Contrariwise, if political parties always nominated stellar candidates, reflecting high levels of moral, political, and economic wisdom, then the choice of an electoral system might be less consequential. Since political parties tend to nominate candidates that serve party interests, despite their claims that these interests are identical with the interests of broader society, the poor quality of candidates that political parties nominate is one reason to support the abolition of political parties.[4]

As noted in Section 3.3, two of the mechanisms that political parties themselves use in selecting candidates can also be used if political parties are abolished, namely self-recruitment and sponsorship. While the argument in Chapter 3 was focused solely on establishing that political parties do not serve any necessary function that cannot be served by other means, the argument here will expand that scope to consider whether there are better means for recruiting candidates than these two mechanisms. Indeed, there are reasons to think that these two mechanisms may not be sufficient to ensure that the electorate is presented a choice among high quality candidates.

Self-recruitment depends upon the ambition of individuals to present themselves as candidates for office. While ambition itself does not necessarily compromise the quality of a candidate, nor does it provide a reliable indicator of quality either. A candidate may have ambitions for office that have nothing to do with the proper execution of that office and may be entirely self-serving. On the other hand, the best candidate for office might be someone who has no ambitions for that office whatsoever. One need not appeal here to Plato's conception of reluctant philosopher kings who believe "that while still living they have been transported to the Islands of the Blessed" (Plato, 1961, p. 751 [519c]) and therefore are unwilling to descend from such lofty heights to be sullied by engagement in political affairs. A worthy candidate may simply

---

[4]See the arguments in Chapter 2, particularly those of Ostrogorski, who provides ample support for this claim in his study.

be engaged in other endeavors and may never have considered serving in public office as a viable career option.

Sponsorship without political parties is a problematic mechanism in the same way that it is problematic with political parties. It is special interests that typically sponsor candidates for office, perhaps special interests in the form of an organization such as a pressure group or a political action committee. Such candidates are indeed be expected to serve those special interests, and if only candidates sponsored by special interests powerful enough to maintain such organizations are offered in an election, then there will be many public interests that may not be represented at all by candidates on the ballot. It is possible that sponsored candidates might incidentally represent more than just the special interests that sponsored them, but sponsorship does not seem to be a reliable mechanism for ensuring that a wide range of public interests are properly represented in the candidates for office. In fact, there may be a better chance that a political party would nominate a candidate that represents broad public interests than a special interest would.

One possibility for recruitment that has emerged fairly recently is a mechanism for soliciting nominations for candidates directly from the electorate. For example, perhaps a newspaper might request letters to the editor recommending individuals who would be good candidates for office. Based on that input, the newspaper might conduct a subsequent poll to gauge what support the recommended individuals might have from the electorate. One could imagine that a non-profit organization might also perform this function using a wider range of information technologies, or even a governmental agency that manages the elections, if it could be ensured that the agency in question would not abuse that function by manipulating the process. Yet if that agency is entrusted with managing the elections, any checks and balances that ensure that elections are conducted fairly should be able to be applied to the nomination of candidates as well.

Such a process may still be subject to abuse, regardless of which organization or institution conducts the process. One could imagine a particularly ambitious individual organizing followers to submit a nomination and to solicit support in the polls to make it seem that the individual was compelled by public acclaim to be a candidate for office, whereas the candidacy was always motivated

4.2. RECRUITMENT OF CANDIDATES

by simple ambition. A special interest group might do the same to promote a candidate favorable its interests. Yet such abuse would not be significantly different from current processes related to self-recruitment and sponsorship, though the current processes seem somewhat more honest in their manifestations of ambition. What the proposed new process would offer is at least the possibility that a candidate who had not considered serving in public office may be nominated by members of the community, thereby offering the electorate more options on the ballot than would otherwise have been presented.

Of course, the individuals nominated by such a process would need to agree to be candidates for office. It does not seem reasonable to force a person to appear as a candidate on a ballot and possibly to serve in office if elected, as Plato imagined that the philosopher kings would be forced. Nor should it displace other methods for recruitment of candidates. Furthermore, there would still be legal requirements that need to be met in order to appear on the ballot that might not be met despite an initial nomination from members of the community. The point that I am arguing here is that there is an alternative mechanism besides self-nomination and sponsorship that could be considered and pursued to ensure that voters are presented with high quality candidates for office and that do not depend upon political parties. I have discussed one suggestion here. Better options may be proposed once more people start thinking of how elections might better be conducted without political parties.

Another issue that should be mentioned in this context is that political parties seem to serve another function besides the ones discussed in Chapter 3, albeit an indirect function. Political parties also seem to limit the number of viable candidates on a ballot, thereby reducing the cognitive requirements on voters in casting votes. This alleged function seems to be a rather dubious one, and I think it was properly omitted from the discussion in Chapter 3, but it does raise a practical concern regarding the conduct of elections without political parties. Perhaps indeed a two-party system provides insufficient choice for voters to decide how a community, region, or nation is governed, for example, but if, in the absence of political parties, voters were confronted with hundreds of candidates on a ballot, the act of voting may become prohibitively demanding such that voter participation actually decreases from levels under political parties.[5]

Legal requirements for appearing on a ballot will control the number of candidates to some extent, for example, by requiring potential candidates to submit a petition signed by certain number of eligible voters.[6] Such a requirement would limit the number of possible candidates to the total number of eligible voters divided by the number of signatures required on each petition, since most requirements of this sort demand that each eligible voter may sign only one such petition for each office. Still, the number of candidates on a ballot may indeed increase significantly for many offices in the absence of the efforts of political parties to restrict the options available to voters in their favor.

Yet perhaps the problem here is not specifically the number of candidates on the ballot, but the way that the vote is structured on the ballot, if there are no party labels on the ballot to help voters choose which candidate to select.[7] I will discuss this issue more generally in terms of informing voters.

4.3 Informing Voters

In discussing the function of structuring the vote in Section 3.1, it was noted that there are alternate ways to structure the vote without using labels of political parties. There it was suggested that candidates might be ranked according to how liberal or conservative they are, whether the candidate provides such a ranking or some third-party organization does based on an evaluation of the candidates' positions. For my part, I am opposed to this kind of one-dimensional ranking, which levels off the complexity of the possibilities of political opinions in order to align

---

[5]This situation would be problematic, indeed, if high levels of voter participation is a desired goal, which it is not the case for everyone, such as Jason Brennan, for example. See (Brennan, 2012) and (Brennan, 2017).

[6]Current requirements for the number of signatures on each petition are typically influenced by political parties seeking to reduce the competition from independent candidates, so such requirements would likely need to be revisited upon the abolition of political parties.

[7]Although the number of candidates may still be a concern in some cases, particularly in the United States, where voters are commonly asked to vote on a larger number of offices and ballot measures than in other countries, in which voters may only be voting for a member of the legislature or for a president in any given election.

4.3. INFORMING VOTERS

to an overly simplistic measure. Since I am opposed to such one-dimensional thinking under the influence of political parties, still less am I willing to countenance it if political parties were to be abolished, which would substitute the tyranny of an abstraction for the corruption of a concrete thing.

The reason for structuring votes with the labels of political parties or a ranking on a scale from liberal to conservative is presumably to help voters decide how to vote among a potentially large list of candidates for any given political office. Yet one might expect more from voters than a choice based simply on a mere set of labels or even a ranking. If one accepts a direct connection between rights and responsibilities,[8] then the right to vote entails a correlative responsibility on the part of each voter, which I claim to be the responsibility to be informed about the choices that are presented on the ballot, as well as the consequences for selecting each option over the others. Attempting to make the choices of voters easier by providing shortcuts on the ballot in the form of political party labels or even rankings on a scale tends to compromise voters' responsibilities to be informed, since labels or rankings can never sufficiently represent the political complexity associated with any given candidate or ballot measure, and does not provide any information at all concerning the consequences of the choice to be made.[9]

The key question is thus not how best to structure the vote on a ballot, but how best to inform voters about the choices they are asked to make. Such choices seem to require significant preparation prior to being presented with a ballot to complete. Many voting districts provide voters with a sample ballot in advance of the day of an election, and some provide voters the option to complete an absentee ballot, both of which provide voters the opportunity prior to voting to consider all of the candidates for all of the offices on the ballots, some of whom may not have received any publicity in the media outlets to which the voter had access, as well as

---

[8] See Chapter 13 on the connection between rights and responsibilities operative here.

[9] Moreover, I claim that if a candidate can in fact properly be represented by some label or ranking, that if the candidate will always take the most liberal or the most conservative stance, whatever the issue may be, that alone is sufficient evidence to reject the candidate. Political realities can never be decided in the public interest in such a simplistic way.

any ballot measures or propositions that the voter will be asked to approve or reject. Such provisions seem necessary in order to give voters sufficient time and information to research the options that are presented on the ballot before actually casting any votes.[10]

Yet this level of advance information is not sufficient in itself, if the voter cannot get additional information about the candidates or the ballot measures in order to make an informed choice. While the opportunities for finding information perhaps have never been greater, and additional information channels will likely be developed in the future, this proliferation of possibilities for finding information has also proliferated propaganda and misinformation, and there is no reason to think that the abolition of political parties will eliminate such misinformation and propaganda, though it may possibly be reduced to some extent.

Propaganda and misinformation are problems whether political parties are abolished or not, so I set aside such issues from consideration here, except to note that they ought to be addressed in conjunction with efforts to provide additional capabilities to voters to research ballot options prior to casting a vote.

One piece of information that ought not to be problematic is the duties of the office that voters are asked to elect. If I am asked on a ballot to choose between several candidates for the office of County Clerk, I need to understand what a County Clerk does in order to decide which of the candidates is most qualified to serve in that office. A committed partisan may not feel the need for that level of understanding, since such a partisan will tend simply to choose whatever candidate is associated with the partisan's political party. In the absence of political parties, this understanding of each political office becomes more important, as voters need to evaluate not just the characters of the candidates on the ballots, but the ability of each candidate to serve the functions of the office in question.

Access to information about political offices should not be controversial, though it may not be easy in every case to find that information. Yet there may be some mismatch in certain cases between understanding what the duties of a particular office may be and understanding what qualities a candidate should have in

---

[10]See also (Kroh, 2009) which argues that even ideological voting requires a level of sophistication on the part of voters.

order to serve in that office well. I raise this issue here, since for one category of political office, those qualities may be understood quite differently once political parties are abolished. Here I am thinking of a legislator, who will clearly need to operate differently in the absence of political parties than under a party system. This will be the topic of the following chapter, in which the question of informing voters will be revisited once the conduct of this office is reconsidered.

Chapter 5

The New Legislators

One argument in favor of political parties that has not been considered yet is that without political parties to aggregate interests, specifically the interests of representatives, the legislature and the resulting overall government will be unstable, chaotic, and indecisive, resulting in gridlock. Ware claims that "the absence of parties in legislative chambers can lead to incoherence in policymaking" (Ware, 1987, p. 63). Schattschneider also takes this position (Schattschneider, 2017, pp. 192–193), which clearly underlies his claim "that modern democracy is unthinkable save in terms of the parties" (Schattschneider, 2017, p. 1). If valid, this argument would pose a serious objection to the main argument of this study.

As noted in Chapter 2, Robert Michels argues that however democratic the principles of a political party may be, in its operation a political party will inevitably devolve into an oligarchy (Michels, 1915). Perhaps Michels' "Iron Law of Oligarchy" is correct, not merely with regard to the particular political parties he studied at the time, but with regard to all political parties, and that it is this party oligarchy that is responsible for the stability of democratic legislatures by virtue of the imposition of party discipline on legislators affiliated with those parties to carry out the policies dictated by the party oligarchy.

Suppose that all of this is correct. What would this indicate about modern democracies? Legislatures are fundamental institutions of democratic governments. If legislatures and their resulting governments cannot function without party discipline to stabilize them, and political parties inevitably become oligarchic in their operation, then the conclusion seems to be that modern democracies are fundamentally a fiction, that the apparent democracy is a mere veneer laid overtop institutions and processes that cannot be democratic in order to function. If such is the case, then perhaps the best course of action would be to abandon the pretense of democracy altogether and explicitly to adopt a form of government that adequately represents the ways in which modern governments must function.

However, one may wonder whether it is indeed correct that democratic legislatures and governments cannot operate effectively without the discipline of political parties. Perhaps this observation is dependent on the maturity of the democracy in question. There may be evidence that early democracies devolved into indecisive chaos without political parties, but that situation may have been a reflection of the level of development of modern democracy and not a necessary feature of all modern democracies. Just because early democracies experienced problems does not mean that more mature democracies must experience the same problems.

Where such problems continue to occur, it may be questioned to what extent political parties themselves contribute to the problems. If a partisan environment already exists, and an opportunity is presented for non-partisan deliberation which only devolves into chaos and indecision, due precisely to the introduction of specifically partisan disagreements, that does not mean that political parties are therefore necessary to provide stability. Rather, it was the underlying partisanship that was responsible for the problems in the first place.

This study will not give up on democracy quite yet. The abolition of political parties must be accompanied by measures that help reduce the tendency toward partisanship that would lead to the development of political parties. Without such measures, political parties will merely rise again from the grave, whether in explicit form or as shadow organizations. It is not clear whether such measures could simply be implemented in the form of constitutional provisions, since there is a strong tendency for people to gravitate toward political parties, as some have noted.[1] In what follows, I will argue that the place to start is with the practice of leg-

---

[1] Such as (Schattschneider, 2017, p. 52).

islators and therefore with the expectations of the function of legislators when voters choose their representatives in a legislature. If partisanship can be suppressed in legislators, then there is a possibility that it may be suppressed in the broader electorate, thereby resulting in a fully democratic government free of the influences of political parties.

5.1 Ostrogorski's Temporary Parties

As noted in Section 2.2, Ostrogorski develops a line of criticism against political parties based on an extensive study of the development and subsequent functioning of political parties both in Great Britain (Ostrogorski, 1902a) and the United States (Ostrogorski, 1902b). The core of the problems that Ostrogorski catalogs regarding political parties is the level of organization on which parties increasingly rely, ultimately becoming an effective machine. Anticipating the arguments presented in Section 2.3, Ostrogorki notes with regard to the organization in party formalism, "The play of its machinery, which is necessarily uniform and rigid, reduces opinion to a dead level" (Ostrogorski, 1902b, p. 651). Furthermore, the development of the machinery of a political party requires a level of internal bureaucracy dependent upon a class of professionals who gain considerable influence within the party, sometimes exploiting such influence for private rather than public benefit.

> The more perfect the organization at the disposal of party convention is, the better it accomplishes these results, that is to say, the more it demoralizes the party and lowers public life. But, on the other hand, to maintain themselves, the parties have more and more need of a strong organization, which alone can make up for the nullity of the convention on which they rest. The upshot, then, is a vicious circle. (Ostrogorski, 1902b, p. 651)

Whereas Weil and I consider the problems with political parties sufficient to merit the abolition of all political parties, this is not Ostrogorski's response. Rather, he proposes a means whereby he believes that a political party can "be restored to its proper function" (Ostrogorski, 1902b, p. 652).

Ostrogorski identifies a confusion regarding the proper function of political parties, "between party conceived as a combination of free citizens pursuing a political object, and party as a troop storming the heights of power in order to divide the spoils" (Ostrogorski, 1902b, p. 653). The evils that political parties have engendered, as Ostrogorski has extensively documented in his study of political parties in Great Britain and the United States and as summarized in Section 2.2, "necessarily spring from the exercise of power proposed as the end and aim of party" (Ostrogorski, 1902b, p. 656).

What Ostrogorski considers to be an obvious solution, rather than abolishing political parties, "consist[s] in discarding the use of permanent parties with power as their end, and in restoring and reserving to party its essential character of a combination of citizens formed specially for a particular political issue" (Ostrogorski, 1902b, p. 658).

> Party as a general contractor for the numerous and varied problems present and to come, awaiting solution, would give place to special organizations, limited to particular objects. It would cease to be a medley of groups and individuals united by a fictitious agreement, and would constitute an association, the homogeneity of which would be ensured by its single aim. Party holding its members, once they have joined it, in a vice-like grasp would give place to combinations forming and re-forming spontaneously, according to the changing problems of life and the play of opinion brought about thereby. Citizens who part company on one question would join forces on another. (Ostrogorski, 1902b, p. 658)

Ostrogorski grounds this proposal on the need for parties to focus on one issue at a time. "Those who have conducted election campaigns among the masses are unanimous on this point, they all agree that it is impossible to make the electors understand more than one question at a time, but that, on the other hand, if one deals with a single problem and takes trouble — one must take a

5.1. OSTROGORSKI'S TEMPORARY PARTIES

great deal — to explain it well, one can drive it into the popular mind" (Ostrogorski, 1902b, p. 660). Consequently, he proposes that *ad hoc* parties form prior to an election around different sides of a single issue, enabling voters essentially to decide the issue by electing the party representing the preferred side to the legislature. Once in power, the elected legislators of the prevailing political party would then implement the required legislation according to the mandate of the electorate, and then the parties would be disbanded and new parties formed around a different issue for the next election.

Anticipating a number of concerns, Ostrogorski defends his proposal against a series of objections,[2] including:

- that permanent political parties will be more efficient than *ad hoc* organizations for different purposes (Ostrogorski, 1902b, p. 682);

- that "the existence of several organizations for different objects [would] be a source of confusion" (Ostrogorski, 1902b, p. 682);

- that it would be difficult to manage the political issues that are presented to the public without permanent organizations (Ostrogorski, 1902b, pp. 683–684);

- that "the national thought and will [would] undergo a sort of frittering away, destructive of those general views which secure consistency in purpose and order in political action, which assign to each problem its time and place, according to the predominant needs and aspirations of the nation" (Ostrogorski, 1902b, p. 684);

- that voters prefer to have positions on all possible issues bundled together, rather than considering them one at a time (Ostrogorski, 1902b, p. 685);

- that representatives would become mere delegates appointed to implement particular positions as indicated by the electorate (Ostrogorski, 1902b, p. 686);

---

[2]Additionally, Ostrogorski argues against Rousseau's conception of the general will, substituting a competing conception that is more consonant with his proposal for temporary political parties (Ostrogorski, 1902b, pp. 674–675). For my thoughts on Rousseau's general will, see Chapter 12.

- that it would be difficult "to recruit political parties, and to train men to lead them, without the allurement of power" (Ostrogorski, 1902b, p. 686);

Ostrogorski's defense against all of these objections and any others that may be devised is to provide a summary response: "the existing system is collapsing, and from the ruin and disorder accumulated by it the new method is already emerging, as a human being comes into the world amid the throes of childbirth" (Ostrogorski, 1902b, p. 687), and this new method consists of citizens forming temporary organizations such as voter leagues to enact ballot measures and constitutional amendments, essentially bypassing the elected members of political parties under the current system (Ostrogorski, 1902b, pp. 689–690). Ostrogorski's proposal merely formalizes the trend that was already emerging.

Yet voter leagues have not developed into the kind of temporary parties that Ostrogorski imagined that they would. Rather, political parties have survived the backlash against the kind of brutal political machines that existed at the end of the 19th century as documented by Ostrogorski and have evolved in different ways. Some criticisms of political parties may have diminished their force somewhat, whereas others have been intensified as a result of this evolution.[3] Still, I think the criticisms of political parties reviewed in Chapter 2 will remain pertinent so long as political parties persist as permanent organizations, which Ostrogorski clearly recognizes and which my own arguments emphasize. Whereas Ostrogorski thinks that such organizations can be reformed by making them merely temporary, I think that their status as organizations itself makes them persistently problematic.

In particular, I think Ostrogorski's proposal contains three fatal flaws:

1. Perhaps the electorate in Ostrogorski's time could only track one political issue at a time, but that does not seem to be the case with subsequent electorates. Even if individual voters would prefer to focus on one issue at a time, multiple issues

---

[3] Indeed, should this book be read in the future, and political parties have not yet been abolished, I expect that political parties will have evolved in still different ways. Consequently, it would merely represent a historical footnote were I to evaluate the state of political parties at the time of writing, which I will not do.

5.1. OSTROGORSKI'S TEMPORARY PARTIES

continue to be posed to voters such that they are obliged to consider all of them when voting in an election regardless of any alleged preferences.

2. It is not clear that a nation or a community can wait until the next election to decide an issue other than the single one on which Ostrogorki's temporary parties were based. Any government will be facing multiple issues at any given time, and if members of a legislature were elected from temporary parties consolidated around positions regarding a single issue, those legislators would still be obliged to debate and to decide those other issues, even though they are aligned to party organizations formed on a single issue different than the remaining issues that need to be decided. The resulting legislative actions may therefore not represent the intentions of the electorate as a whole for those other issues compared to the actions that may have been enacted if the temporary parties had been formed around a different issue, as Ostrogorski himself recognizes (Ostrogorski, 1902b, p. 660).

3. There is no guarantee or even incentive for temporary parties to disband after creating effective organizations that won an election and passed legislation on a single issue. In fact, there is incentive for a temporary party that did not win a election to remain organized in order to win the next election and to repeal the legislation that a competing party may have been able to enact. These factors seem to be critically responsible for the formation of modern political parties in Great Britain and the United States based on the single issues that originally characterized them. Consequently, there seem to be strong incentives for temporary parties to retain their organization not only to continue to fight for the original issues on which they were formed, but also to apply that organization to new issues, thus resulting in the same kind of permanent political parties that Ostrogorski criticizes.

Consequently, Ostrogorski's proposal seems too strongly based on political trends at the time he wrote, which do not seem to be relevant to the continuing problems fostered subsequently by political parties.

5.2 Toward a New Practice for Legislators

There is a very attractive aspect of Ostrogorski's proposal that seems relevant to the abolition of political parties, even if the proposal as a whole does not seem viable. If political parties are merely temporary, then Ostrogorski notes that "Citizens who part company on one question would join forces on another" (Ostrogorski, 1902b, p. 658). According to Ostrogorski's proposal, once the question for which the current set of temporary political parties is decided and a new set of temporary political parties is organized around another question, citizens who previously found themselves opponents may later find themselves allies. Knowing that this will be a possibility in the future, citizens who are aligned to the current set of political parties should therefore avoid alienating or demonizing members of opposing parties, thereby fostering a greater sense of cooperation in discussing the current question at hand.

Indeed, many legislators already find themselves in the same position, even under party systems, where by previous experience they know that they may need for some future issue the support of legislators who currently oppose them on a current issue. Accordingly, they may be willing to concede points on that current issue in order to gain political capital that can be expended in the future. This is part of a familiar pattern of political negotiation. Likewise, if Ostrogorski's proposal were feasible, and political parties were merely temporary, then it would be expected that such negotiations across party lines would become more commonplace, thereby reducing polarization within the legislature.

Yet if political parties were abolished outright, rather than being made temporary, this pattern would be expected to be even more common, since in that case legislators would simply find themselves on one or other side of a given issue, without the artificial organizational pressures that come with political parties. In that instance, legislators should more easily be able to cooperate with opposing sides to come to a mutually beneficial resolution, or even to be persuaded to reconsider their side on an issue. Thus, Weil claims that upon the abolition of political parties, "Elected politicians would associate and disassociate following the natural and changing flow of affinities. I may very well agree with Mr A on the question of colonialism, yet disagree with him on the issue of agrarian ownership, and my relations with Mr B may be the exact reverse" (Weil, 2014, p. 29).

A legislator represents a particular constituency. The notion of representation in this case can entail some ambiguity for some, where representation can be understood in the sense of the representation embodied within a painting, whereby it might be said that a subject within the painting is represented well or poorly, to the extent that the painting presents the subject according to how the subject appears in actuality. In this way, a member of a minority class within a society might complain that the composition of the legislature does not properly represent the society as a whole, meaning that there are too many members of a majority class and not enough of the minority class who are elected as legislators.[4]

While I am sympathetic to the justice of such complaints, for my part, as a white male, I would much rather have a competent black woman serving as the representative for the constituency in which I reside rather than an incompetent white man. Nor does the conception of representation as a reflection of the racial, ethnic, or sexual composition of the broader society within the legislature seem particularly relevant to the question of the abolition of political parties. Political parties as such have not been instrumental in championing this form of representation, and the abolition of political parties would not guarantee such representation either. Accordingly, the conception of representation in the discussion that follows relates to the primary function of a legislator in drafting legislation and in casting votes on behalf of the members of the constituency and not to the composition of a legislature.

Yet even given this sense of representation, there are competing conceptions of what it means for a legislator to represent the constituency and more particularly the voters who elected that legislator. Citing Burke's speech to the electors of Bristol (Burke, 1777, pp. 352–355), Farrell describes this as a difference between a representative "as a *delegate* of the voters, or as a *trustee*" (Farrell, 2001, p. 170):

> According to the first type, MPs are said to listen closely to the views of the voters. There are even suggestions that they are 'mandated' by the voters to take

---

[4]See (Pitkin, 1967) for an extensive discussion on various conceptions of representation.

certain decisions. According to the second type, the trustee role — favoured by Burke — MPs are elected to act on behalf of the constituency as a whole. They are better placed than anyone to weigh up the often conflicting views of their voters and come to a considered decision, without needing to always check back with the voters. (Farrell, 2001, p. 171)

Under Ostrogorski's recommendation for temporary political parties, since those parties have been organized around a single issue, the delegate conception of a representative is the most appropriate one, as noted in one of the objections he lists. If voters have elected a representative from a political party, it is because in aggregate they prefer the position on the issue adopted by that political party. In that case, the representative owes it to the voters to ensure that votes in the legislature are cast in accordance with that preference.

Yet I argued in Section 5.1 above that Ostrogorski's proposal is flawed, in part because a legislature must attend to more than one issue at any given time. Therefore, voters must elect representatives based on their positions on multiple questions. Just as political parties cannot represent the full range of possible positions that individual voters may hold, as argued in Section 2.3, nor can the set of candidates on the ballot for a particular legislative seat represent the full range of possible positions, whether those candidates are aligned to political parties or not. As a consequence, voters must decide which candidate most closely represents their interests, though no candidate may perfectly endorse all of the positions that an individual voter holds. The candidate that is ultimately elected, therefore, cannot assume that the electorate fully endorses all of the positions that the candidate holds by virtue of receiving more votes than any other candidate, assuming a plurality or majoritarian electoral system. For some given issue, it may be that the majority of voters strongly opposes the candidate's position on that issue, but that a majority of voters cast a vote for the candidate based on that candidate's positions on other issues. The result is that the representative cannot properly identify any mandate from the voters on any given issue, and because of this, voters cannot properly claim that the representative has a mandate to take particular actions with regard to any given issue, based on

5.2. TOWARD A NEW PRACTICE FOR LEGISLATORS

what factors were most important to each individual voter in casting a vote. Consequently, the delegate conception of a representative cannot be sustained.

Surely Burke is correct here. He claims, "Your representative owes you, not his industry only, but his judgment; and he betrays, instead of serving you, if he sacrifices it to your opinion" (Burke, 1777, p. 353). Yet by the same measure, the representative cannot properly apply a merely partisan judgment, by assuming that the electorate has given the representative any mandate to enact all of the policies endorsed by the political party under which the representative ran as a candidate, for the same reasons as were argued in the last paragraph. The representative represents all members of the constituency, not only those who voted for the representative, still less only those who endorse all of the policies proposed by the representative's political party.

After a particularly contentious election, one sometimes hears the elected representative promising that he or she will represent all of the constituency, not just those who voted for the representative. This ought always to be the case, although in such circumstances it is rare that this promise has any practical implications. Rather, the elected representative tends to represent all of the constituency as though they were supporters of the representative's political party, ultimately ignoring the opinions of those who voted for someone else. Yet the right of a representative to cast a vote within the legislature on behalf of the entire constituency entails the responsibility to ensure that the vote serves the interests of the entire constituency as best as possible. This responsibility therefore indicates that the representative will need to make compromises.

The word 'compromise' has become tarnished, mainly by conflating the different senses of the word. Certainly a representative may compromise his or her integrity by taking certain actions, even by failing to honor a campaign promise. Yet if that promise does not serve the interests of the entire constituency, but only a part of it, then such a campaign promise should not have been made in the first place. Making compromises in order to pass legislation is part of the business of a legislature, even if one endorses strong political parties. As Schattschneider notes, "It is idle to talk as if parties would not find it necessary to compromise if politicians were sufficiently high-minded. To refuse to make concessions and to refuse to develop a many-sided program is simply to refuse to make a bid for power" (Schattschneider, 2017, p. 62). Furthermore, in order to serve the interests of the entire constituency, the representative ought properly to seek compromises in passing legislation even if the majority of legislators hold an extreme position on the issue at hand, specifically to honor the responsibility to serve the interests of the entire constituency, as well as the entire nation, state, or province. This is the judgment that the representative owes.

Yet the usual conception of compromise as making concessions or splitting the difference with regard to some issue is not the only way to understand the way in which a legislator may represent the competing interests of the constituency that the legislator represents. Accordingly, Mary Parker Follett makes a distinction between compromise and what she calls "integrating interests" (Follett, 1924, p. 42), which she counts as a third way of addressing a conflict, different from domination, in which one party gains a victory at the expense of the other party, or compromise, in which both parties give up something (Follett, 1918, pp. 26–27) (Follett, 1924, pp. 45–46). Rather, the strategy of integrating interests seeks new solutions that may maximize the gains of both parties to the conflict. "The moment you try to integrate loss, you reduce loss; as when you try to integrate gain, you increase gain" (Follett, 1924, p. 45). Follett provides a few examples of this pattern of integrating interests, such as:

> Take the Workmen's Compensation Act; the active cooperation between employers and workmen to carry out this law shows its value to both. The employer has the following advantages: he had formerly to pay much more when the employee's lawyer succeeded in winning the case than he pays now; and there was an uncertainty hanging over a business that might be wiped out if a serious accident occurred. On the other hand, the employees under the old system either did not get anything if the other side won, or even if they themselves won, they had to wait a long time for the award and payment, when it was at the moment of the injury or illness that they needed the money. Since the negligence of fellow-workmen has been in-

> cluded, the employee has been fully protected. This is a good example of the integrating of individual interests. (Follett, 1924, p. 44)

If it is possible, Follett's conception of integrating interests seems to be the proper approach for a legislator to ensure that the interests of all constituents in the legislator's district are promoted, rather than only those constituents who voted for the legislator.

However, there may be issues in which interests simply cannot be fully integrated, for example, cases in which finite resources must be allocated, and increasing allotments to some constituents means decreasing allotments to others. In such cases, it seems that compromise of some form is required. Consequently, after legislators have completed their deliberative work, and a piece of legislation is submitted to the broader legislature for a vote, the sponsors of the legislation should explain to the entire legislature and to their constituents the rationale for the final form of the legislation, why the particular compromise was adopted within the legislation rather than some other compromise or integration of interests. In any case, if the legislator is to represent all constituents, then it seems that the legislator has the responsibility to seek either integration of interests or compromise regarding all issues that come before the legislature, rather than seeking to dominate an opposing side, which is typically the primary tactic adopted under pressure from political parties.

If this indeed is the responsibility that legislators should honor, then candidates for a seat in a legislature ought to campaign accordingly, even under a system of political parties. Yet the organizational pressures of political parties tend to suppress any willingness to compromise or even to integrate interests. The reason that a political party endorses candidates for office is to ensure that the party is in a strong position to enact its policies, so it will not welcome a candidate who campaigns under a commitment to compromise and therefore possibly to undermine those policies. If a candidate is not inclined to make a promise to enact the political party's policies on a given issue, perhaps because the candidate does not completely agree with those policies, the candidate may try to remain silent on the issue. However, the pressures to differentiate a candidate from political opponents will tend to force candidates toward endorsing some position that opposes the position endorsed by an opponent, and the easiest position to endorse is the position held by the candidate's political party, with a promise to enact the party's policies, thus tending toward full alignment of candidates to political parties. Once elected, then, the representative is expected to honor that promise, else the representative risks being accused of compromising his or her integrity, with the inevitable result that the interests of some constituents are not properly served.

On the abolition of political parties, though, there would be no such organizational pressure, from political parties at least, to align to a certain set of policies, so campaigns can be conducted differently. As Weil writes, "At elections, candidates would tell voters not, 'I wear such and such a label' — which tells the public nearly nothing as regards their actual position on actual issues — but rather, 'My views are such and such on such and such important problem'" (Weil, 2014, p. 29). Indeed, candidates would be able to declare their views more openly in the absence of political parties.

However, I think publicizing a candidate's views is insufficient, if the candidate will have a responsibility to integrate interests or to compromise effectively to support the interests of the entire constituency once elected, as I have argued. While the electorate certainly needs to know where the candidate stands on any given issue as a starting position, it also needs to know how the candidate is planning to legislate if elected. In other words, the electorate needs to know exactly how the candidate will think and function in office if that candidate becomes a member of the legislature. If the candidate is the incumbent of the office, then the electorate should already have some evidence of how their representative is already performing in office, but such a candidate would do well to remind the electorate, particularly since many of them will not be following the votes in the legislature and may not have sufficient information to know how the representative actually functions. If the candidate has never held office, then that candidate certainly owes the electorate some account of what to expect from the candidate if they elect that candidate to the legislature.

Thus, I think each candidate should start campaigning by declaring how the candidate would proceed to address a particular issue, if the candidate had complete freedom to enact policies in accordance with the candidate's preference and conscience. This would give the electorate an idea of the candidate's character as an

5.2. TOWARD A NEW PRACTICE FOR LEGISLATORS   121

initial point of reference. Next the candidate should indicate the extent to which the candidate would integrate interests or would compromise on that issue, if elected, beyond that candidate's personal position on the issue. The candidate might outline a range of alternatives that would be acceptable, possibly ranking the alternatives in order of preference. Alternatively, the candidate might describe some conditions that the candidate would be seeking in any possible compromise. If each candidate campaigned accordingly, then the electorate would be able to cast votes not merely on the basis of how closely the positions adopted by particular candidates matched their own positions on important issues, but also on how far each voter could trust a particular candidate's political judgment, in accordance with Burke's conception of what a representative owes the constituency, in deciding not only the issues on which the candidate campaigned, but also any new issues that may emerge during the representative's term of office.

Of course, once elected it would be expected that the representative will actually function within the legislature as described in the campaign. Without political parties to keep representatives aligned to party lines, those representatives would likely align themselves according to the sides they adopt regarding particular issues, where the alignment of sides on one issue should be expected to be quite different with regard to other issues, undermining the tendencies to form permanent parties. Since an opposing legislator on one issue may be a supporting legislator on another issue, the incentives would be much higher for legislators to integrate interests or to compromise productively to seek a solution serving the interests of all of the representatives' constituencies, as Ostrogorski suggested in his proposal for temporary parties, but operative within a single legislative session rather than subsequent ones, and without the organizational pressures of political parties to remain aligned to the same political divisions across multiple issues.

The focus in this chapter has been on legislators representing a constituency, but similar patterns of campaigning and compromising should apply to other elected offices, such as governors or presidents. Without political parties to align political debate to party lines, each candidate for any office owes an account to the electorate of how that candidate would function in office, whether in voting on legislation in the case of legislators, or in proposing policies and directing government offices in the case of executives.

It may be objected that these proposals seem highly optimistic and improbable, but this reaction may simply be the reflection of long familiarity with the current systems of political parties and the patterns of campaigning and governance that they entail. If political parties are indeed abolished, then the conduct of campaigns and the practice of legislators in office must change from the patterns seen under political parties, else there is a strong likelihood that political parties may simply reappear in a different guise, with no improvement in the overall political situation. I have argued for patterns of conduct that appear to be owed to the constituencies of representatives even under systems of political parties, but which seem to be compromised precisely by those parties. In the absence of political parties, these are precisely the patterns that I claim the electorate needs to demand from any candidate for office and needs to see in the conduct of representatives within a legislature if those representatives want to be returned to office after the next election.

If it is objected that these expectations are impossible,[5] then perhaps the pretense of democracy ought thereby to be abandoned. The only alternative cannot be to surrender the operation of democracy to political parties and to accept the consequences, however adverse. If political parties are not serving the people, and democracy cannot function without political parties, then it seems therefore that alternatives to democracy should be considered. For my part, I think that democracy without political parties is not only possible, but optimal, and that democratic legislatures can operate under the patterns outlined in this chapter.

---

[5]For example, Ware claims that "The nineteenth-century ideal of the independent minded representative, who weighs up the arguments and reaches a considered judgement, is a chimera" (Ware, 1987, p. 60).

Chapter 6
Conclusion

Political parties are organizations, but strange ones. They seem to function equally as organizations and as abstractions. They are organizations with very imperfect mechanisms of control, given the variety of influences to which they respond, often in very abstract ways. They are abstractions with very concrete effects, given the party machinery by which they operate as organizations. It seems to be this dual aspect that makes political parties more problematic than other organizations or abstractions, in that they are compounding the problems of each aspect in their combination.

As noted in the Introduction, Burke endorsed political parties, Hume tolerated them, and Bolingbroke opposed them. This investigation sides with Bolingbroke in rejecting political parties. The stages of the argument were as follows:

- Summarize the arguments against political parties offered by Bolingbroke, Ostrogorski, Weil, and others, adding a new series of arguments grounded in the nature of a political party as an organization.

- Consider the functions of political parties to determine whether those functions could be served by institutions other than political parties, or indeed whether those functions need to be served at all.

- With regard to the role that political parties serve in democratic elections, investigate in greater detail how elections might be conducted in the absence of political parties.

- With regard to the role that political parties serve in government, particularly in legislatures, investigate in greater detail how legislators might function in the absence of political parties.

Had political parties served one or more indispensable functions in a democracy that could not be served in some other way, then this investigation might have concluded with Hume that political parties were necessary evils. Yet whatever functions political parties may currently serve, those functions indeed either can be served by other institutions, often in ways more conducive to a healthy democracy than political parties can, or need not be served at all, since those functions primarily serve the interests of political parties, rather than citizens of democracies. The arguments against political parties are sufficiently strong and wide ranging that the abolition of political parties seems fully justified.

Political parties may indeed have been instrumental, even necessary, in the early development of modern democracies. This does not mean that political parties are still necessary today, or even desirable. Democratic societies are not the same as they had been at the instigation of modern democracies, and the understanding of how democratic governments could function effectively is no longer an unknown factor, such that democracy does not need to be mediated by political parties any longer.

In early democracies, the electorate may have required such mediation in order to become effective citizens in a democracy. Citizens may not have been in the habit of participation in a democratic process and may have required the encouragement of political parties to motivate them to go to the polls to cast a vote. Even if they were motivated, they may not have had sufficient awareness of the candidates for office or the political issues that were facing the nation at the time, whether because newspapers were not widely available to them or because literacy levels were too low. These circumstances are no longer the case in modern, well-established democracies.

Furthermore, the effective practice of democratic governance may not have come naturally to those accustomed to serving either as mere subjects or even as courtiers of a king, or indeed as members of a revolutionary group. There may have been a measure of naivety among legislators in early democracies in thinking that it would be sufficient to debate an issue and then to take a vote in order to determine what is best for a nation, such that they may have needed the discipline of political parties in order to understand how varying interests must be negotiated in order to form sufficient coalitions to enact legislation. There has been sufficient experience with the operations of democratic legislatures since then to understand the conditions under which a legislature can be effective and those in which it degenerates into stalemate or chaos.

To continue to judge the value of political parties according to the functions that they have served in the past is to ignore the ways that democracies evolve, full understanding of which requires continual reassessment of the institutions that may sustain or inhibit a healthy democracy. One may indeed acknowledge with gratitude the role that political parties have served in establishing early democracies, but nevertheless recognize that they have outlasted their usefulness and indeed have become factors compromising the practice of genuine democracy. Such is the conclusion that this investigation has reached.

Even when political parties may have been necessary to establish an early democracy, they have always encouraged political inauthenticity among citizens. Rather than fostering genuine debate, political parties tend to seek automatic adherence to a party line among members and adherents, such that they can wield unified political power without risking fragmentation due to the actual differences of opinions within its power base. Rather than aggregating existing interests, political parties tend to aggregate people toward the party's interests.[1] Since political parties are not strictly necessary in modern democracies, a clear course of action would be simply to abolish them and thereby to abolish their pressure toward political inauthenticity.

Simone Weil saw the partisanship surrounding political parties as manifestation of a deeper problem:

> Nearly everywhere — often even when dealing with purely technical problems — instead of thinking, one merely takes sides: for or against. Such a choice replaces the activity of the mind. This is an intellectual

---

[1] As discussed with regard to this alleged function of political parties in Section 3.6.

> leprosy; it originated in the political world and then spread through the land, contaminating all forms of thinking.
>
> This leprosy is killing us; it is doubtful whether it can be cured without first starting with the abolition of all political parties. (Weil, 2014, p. 34)

If Weil is correct that merely taking a side is being substituted for genuine deliberation and evaluation, then she is likewise correct that the first step toward encouraging authentic thinking on political issues is to remove the pressures toward inauthenticity in the form of political parties.

Note that the abolition of political parties does not entail that people should cease taking sides on political issues. According to the distinctions proposed in the Introduction between sides, factions, caucuses, and political parties, summarized in Table 1.1, the arguments in this investigation relate primarily to divisions that constitute or develop into organizations, namely political parties and to some extent caucuses. It is healthy for citizens in a democracy to have differences of opinions and thereby to align themselves to different sides of an issue, even if those differences of opinion result in differing factions, so long as those factions do not develop into persistent organizations that begin to serve their own interests rather than the interests of citizens. Differing sides of an issue and even competing factions may still be elements in the coordination and integration of overall interests within a democracy that serves all citizens, but the fossilization of sides and factions into political parties interferes with such processes of coordination, precisely because organizations will inevitably have interests that do not reduce to the interests of their members.[2]

The conclusion of Duverger's major study acknowledges that "The opponents of 'party systems' will find much ammunition in this book" (Duverger, 1964, p. 422). He asks a series of rhetorical questions:

1. "But would a system without parties be more satisfactory?"

2. "Would opinion be better represented if candidates were to

---

[2] As argued in the book on technology, (Ressler, 2024, pp. 58–62).

present themselves individually before the electorate without it being able really to know their attitudes?"

3. "Would liberty be better preserved if the government found itself faced with only a scattering of individuals not grouped into political formations?" (Duverger, 1964, p. 423).

This study answers Duverger's first question emphatically in the affirmative.

Duverger's second question is clearly biased, presupposing that voters can only know the attitudes of candidates for office through the mediation of political parties. If this presupposition was ever true, it does not seem supportable now, and Section 4.3 investigates a number of ways whereby voters can more easily be informed about the attitudes of candidates for office without relying on the dubious mechanism of party labels for this purpose.

Duverger's third question seems to presuppose that permanent political formations are the only political grouping that can preserve liberty, as though liberty only survives on the basis a struggle between perpetually warring fixed party organizations. It is not clear why such a presupposition should seem even initially compelling. Perhaps indeed liberty requires some conflict in order to ensure that even the slightest compromise of liberty from any side is challenged,[3] but it is hardly clear that conflicts between political parties are fundamentally driven by a desire to preserve liberty, rather than a fundamental desire to gain and to preserve power for the party, as Weil and others have argued. Rather, inspired by Ostrogorski's proposal for temporary political parties, Chapter 5 investigated ways in which conflicts between different perspectives and interests may be preserved, but aligned to sides of specific issues, without being aligned specifically to the rigid power struggles between permanent political parties.

Yet Duverger himself takes an opposite position, arguing for the persistence of political parties on the following grounds:

1. "We are living on a completely artificial notion of democracy forged by lawyers on the basis of eighteenth-century philosophical ideas" (Duverger, 1964, p. 423). "All government is oligarchic: it necessarily implies the domination of the many by a few" (Duverger, 1964, p. 424).

---
[3] See (Mill, 1977).

2. "A regime without parties ensures the permanence of ruling elites chosen by birth, wealth, or position: to ensure admission to the governing oligarchy a man of the people must accomplish a considerable effort to rise above his initial position; he must also work his way up the ladder of middle-class education and lose contact with the class in which he was born. A regime without parties is of necessity a conservative regime" (Duverger, 1964, pp. 425–426).

3. "Democracy is not threatened by the party regime but by present-day trends in party internal organization" (Duverger, 1964, p. 426).

I responds as follows:

1. Our notion of democracy cannot simply be considered *artificial*, since there is no *natural* notion of democracy, certainly not one that emerges only from the interplay of political parties, so Duverger's claim rests upon a vacuous contrast. The notion of democracy predates political parties, and it has been progressively refined since its emergence in ancient Greece, including the contributions of eighteenth-century lawyers. The argument of this book is that political parties have progressively undermined the ideals of democracy, and even if democracy ultimately remains an unattainable ideal,[4] the recommendation here is not to revert to some putatively pure notion of democracy, still less to accept whatever conception of democracy that political parties permit us, but rather that the notion of democracy must be refined further to yield a form of democracy that works without the mediation of political parties. This was the task of Chapters 3, 4, and 5.

2. Duverger's conception of a governing oligarchy seems fundamentally grounded in an old European perspective, one that may not even be operative in Europe any longer, apparently suggesting that democratically oriented politicians must remain uneducated and undeveloped in order to represent their classes. From an American perspective, at least,

---

[4] Like anarchy, as discussed in Chapter 14.

what Duverger describes has long been exactly the ideal for lower and middle classes, namely that one rises above one's initial position precisely by means of education and effort. A politician rising from the lower or middle classes can still represent these classes because nearly everyone in these classes is attempting to do the same, though with varying degrees of success.

Yet it is precisely political parties that have become the governing oligarchies, with the result that the pattern of argument Duverger offers can be thrown back against him in a parallel argument. A man of the people must accomplish a considerable effort to infiltrate the political party organization by endorsing the party line and by accepting party mandates dictated by the current party elites in order to have any political influence. In thus playing the party game, such a man of the people inevitably loses contact with whatever reasons other than ambition and personal advancement he may have had for seeking political influence in the first place.

3. Duverger was aware of Ostrogorski's study, even though Ostrogorski merited mention in Duverger's major book in only two passing references (Duverger, 1964, pp. xxvi, 186), so Duverger should have recognized that the trends in political party organization had been developing for a long time, indeed since their early formations, rather than representing a recent development. I agree that it is precisely the impact of organization that makes political parties problematic, but I deny that it can be remedied with an amendment or correction of the organizational trends, since those problems are inherent in the nature of political parties. Certainly the trends that Duverger noted at the time of his analysis have only continued, despite the evolution of political parties since that time. As noted in Chapter 2, the criticisms of political parties seem to be cumulative, even those that predate the emergence of modern political parties, suggesting that the problems in political parties are endemic, and that additional problems will accrue if political parties are allowed to evolve even further.

However, even if one has accepted the arguments and conclusions in this book, one might claim that the call to abolish political parties is merely a vain proposal that cannot be effected without violence. How will political parties be abolished if political parties hold power in the government? One issue on which competing political parties can agree is that political parties should not be abolished, and therefore any attempt to get legislators belonging to political parties to enact legislation to abolish those political parties is doomed to fail. Political parties will not abolish themselves. Must there be a violent revolution?

Yet one need not aim for legislative or even constitutional abolition of political parties. Rather the goal could be merely *effective abolition*, where political parties are effectively abolished if no one ever votes for them. As La Boétie and Hume noted, political power depends upon continued obedience.[5] The reason that political parties have power is because people continue to vote for them. If voters stop casting their votes in favor of political parties, those parties would vanish. Consequently, the best strategy to implement the abolition of political parties is to aim for effective abolition, by convincing voters to stop voting for candidates aligned to political parties. Let political parties be starved to death.

This is not an easy task, specifically because political parties have become so effective in encouraging political inauthenticity. In many countries, the influence of political parties has undermined the possibility of electing candidates that are not aligned to any political party, convincing large numbers of voters that voting for such candidates would just represent a wasted vote.[6]

Yet a democracy that is not authentic is not democracy at all, where an authentic democracy is one in which the greater part of its citizens exercise political authenticity. If authentic democracy is not possible, then perhaps some other form of government should be established in place of inauthentic putative democracy, rather than merely surrendering to the continued adverse influences of political parties under the pretense of a democracy.[7]

Political parties are only one kind of organization, where orga-

---

[5] See (de la Boétie, 1975) and (Hume, 1987, pp. 32–36).
[6] See Chapter 9 for considerations on the idea of a wasted vote.
[7] It has been noted that "anti-party arguments were once used to undermine systems of representative democracy" (Scarrow, 1996, p. 298). That may have been so. However, I contend that a defense of representative democracy must now include anti-party arguments.

nizations in general were identified as being problematic for authenticity in the book on technology. The reason that political parties were chosen as a target in this investigation was that there was a clear case against them, such that the abolition of this kind of organization would provide a ready solution to the problems that these organizations pose. The situation may not be as clear with other organizations. The same strategy to evaluate political parties may be employed with regard to other kind of organizations, but if those organizations represent necessary evils that cannot simply be abolished, then some way to control the impact of those organizations needs to be devised.[8]

Organizations pose only one challenge to authenticity. The book on technology also identified the cognitive impacts of technology as a factor compromising authentic engagement. This factor will require an additional investigation to determine the scope of its impact, as well as the prospects for regaining authentic engagement not only with technology itself, but also with the broader world to which technology is applied.

Insofar as political parties influence the broader world through the control of governments and in the legislation that establishes or revokes rights and responsibilities, the abolition of political parties and the fostering of political authenticity will surely contribute toward greater authenticity in general. Any step toward authenticity in one domain is a step toward authenticity in all domains.

---

[8]See Chapter 16 for reflections on this topic.

Part II
Topics

Chapter 7

Partisanship in Philosophy

When I was just starting graduate school, I attended a philosophy conference at a nearby university where a rather notable philosopher was scheduled to present a talk. I had liked the work of this philosopher and was interested to hear him in person to see how he practiced philosophy outside of his printed work.

What I noticed soon after he began speaking was that his presentation was not particularly well prepared, but seemed rather to represent improvisations on themes he happened to be thinking about at the time. This kind of talk can also be valuable, particularly to younger philosophers, to see how an established philosopher actually works in preparing material that could eventually be published in a more polished form. However, I was not impressed with the way this particular philosopher presented himself in this context.

He described a thought experiment that he evidently considered to be decisive, but which I found entirely unfounded. Interestingly, he mentioned how he described the thought experiment to his brother, but the brother did not agree with the philosopher's conclusions, upon which the philosopher dismissed his brother's feedback as inconsequential, even though his brother worked in a scientific field not irrelevant to the topic of the thought experiment. For some reason, this dismissal elicited laughter from many in the audience. Later in the talk, in discussing a controversy in his philosophical field, he made a reference to those who disagreed with him, dismissing the opposing view without any argument, but merely alluding to how "right-thinking philosophers" understand the issue. As I looked around the audience, I saw many people smiling and nodding appreciatively, clearly considering themselves among the ranks of "right-thinking philosophers". My poor impression of this particular philosopher was complete when I overheard him speaking rather loudly to someone after the conference session had ended, indicating that he was unavailable the following week, since his wife was having a hysterectomy.

Of the many unpleasant aspects of this talk, the one that bothered me most was the reference to "right-thinking philosophers" in place of any argumentation, with the full acceptance of many audience members. Overall, I had the feeling that I was in a political rally rather than at a philosophy conference. Later, in the elevator as I was leaving the conference, two other attendees, apparently young faculty members of the university that hosted the conference, were commenting on the poor quality of philosophy they had just witnessed, which partly restored my opinion of the present state of philosophy, at least at that university. Interestingly, though, they kept directing furtive glances my way as they spoke. Were they concerned about speaking blasphemy before one of the faithful?

David Hume made the following comment in one of his essays: "But philosophers, who have embraced a party (if that be not a contradiction in terms) ..." (Hume, 1987, p. 469). Hume was writing in an explicitly political context, but I would extend this reflection to partisanship in philosophy. Putative philosophers who embrace some philosophical party seem not to be philosophers to me, at least not very good philosophers.

I am certainly not suggesting that philosophers should never adopt a side with regard to some philosophical issue. Indeed, it seems impossible to practice philosophy without doing so — at least provisionally.[1] However, when those who adopt a side be-

---

[1] One might object that ancient skeptics were able to philosophize without ever taking sides; yet this claim is not supported, for example, by the exposition of Sextus Empiricus, who describes skepticism as "an ability to set out oppositions among things which appear and are thought of in any way at all, an ability by which, because of the equipollence in the opposed objects and accounts, we come first to suspension of judgement and afterwards to tranquility" (Sextus Empiricus, 2000, p. 4). In order to set out oppositions and to determine the equipollence in opposed accounts, it appears necessary at least provisionally to adopt each opposed side in alternation to assess the relative strengths. To start by refusing to accept sides in expectation of skeptical conclusions would be to adopt

gin to function as a faction within a community of philosophers, according to the distinction in the Introduction, then the partisanship that emerges in philosophy may begin to exhibit some of the problems found in political partisanship discussed in Chapter 2, indeed functioning more like a caucus or party.

Yet partisanship in philosophy is hardly a recent phenomenon, since there have been competing schools of philosophy for at least as long as there has been recorded philosophy, notably in the competition between the Academic Skeptics and the Stoics in the Hellenistic period,[2] but going back at least as far as Pythagoras in the Ancient Greek tradition. In Eastern traditions the competition appears to have been even more intense, between Vedic, Jain, and Buddhist schools in India and between Confucian, Taoist, Mohist, and Legalist schools in China, among others, not to mention the competing schools within these broader traditions. Indeed, one might argue that partisanship began precisely with these competing schools in philosophy and then spread to other fields.

It would seem natural for such schools to form and to persist around a particular philosopher, where that philosopher teaches students, and those students would tend to accept those philosophical teachings and to propagate those teachings in turn to their students, long after the original philosopher had died. One of those students might indeed develop doctrines beyond what the original philosopher had taught, in which case a sub-school might develop within that broader philosophical tradition, if the doctrines are still compatible with that broader tradition, but in some cases a completely new school might thereby form. For example, Aristotle broke from the Academy of Plato in which he had been educated to form a new school called the Lyceum, claiming that "piety requires us to honour truth above our friends" (Aristotle, 1984, p. 1732 [1096a16]).

Likewise, it would seem natural for different schools to be in competition with each other. Where the doctrines held by different schools are incompatible, one might demand of each school to defend their doctrines against rival claims. The consequence is that a school not only upholds certain doctrines, but also takes positions against opposing claims and therefore against the rival

---

a dogmatic attitude, which is contrary to Sextus' claim that "the Sceptics are still investigating" (Sextus Empiricus, 2000, p. 3).

[2] (Long, 1986) offers a good overview of this philosophical period.

schools that hold them. This doctrinal competition becomes more acute once rival schools begin to compete for new students or even in some cases for the favor of a ruler or a wealthy sponsor, upon which the survival of the school may depend.

Compared to the proliferation of philosophical schools in the ancient world, the contemporary situation seems far less divisive. Schools as educational institutions are not typically formed around particular philosophers or teachers, but are maintained by nations, provinces, or communities for the broader education of students, and specific philosophical traditions rarely become the basis for the organization of the school, if philosophy is even taught in them at all. Consequentially, the notion of a philosophical school seems to have become largely metaphorical.

However, this educational structure does not mean that partisanship in philosophy has been eliminated. There are still recognizable divisions within contemporary philosophy, most notably between the Analytical and Continental styles or traditions, where it appears that even the standards for philosophy differ between those two broad traditions, with the result that philosophers within one tradition may not be read or even recognized within the other tradition, or so it is typically claimed.

Even within the broader Analytical or Continental traditions, competing schools of thought may be recognized, which is healthy, even necessary for philosophy to survive as a discipline. Alignment around a single set of doctrines collapses into dogmatism, which may be a viable state for some fields, such as the alignment around the Central Dogma in molecular biology concerning the flow of genetic information from DNA to RNA to proteins,[3] but for philosophy such a dogmatic alignment would be fatal.[4]

Yet even if philosophical schools in the contemporary metaphorical sense do not constitute specific organizations, like Plato's Academy or Aristotle's Lyceum, they are supported by institutions like university departments that tend only to hire people who approach the field the same way that members of that department do, or journals and publishers that only publish certain kinds of philosophy, even prizes awarded to those who advance

---

[3] First described in (Crick, 1958). See also (Lorch, 2021, p. 52).

[4] A defense of this blunt statement requires a broader discussion of the nature and methods of philosophy, which will be presented in a forthcoming book on philosophical methodology, tentatively entitled *Perspectival Methodology*.

the way of thinking endorsed by the sponsor of the prize. In this sense, philosophical schools function similarly as highly decentralized political parties, which may be supported by institutions such as newspapers, interest groups, and think tanks.

The popularity of certain schools of thought may push out alternative ways of thinking and alternative approaches to the field. In one sense, this too can be healthy, where unproductive ways of thinking eventually get abandoned in favor of more fruitful approaches. Yet the popularity of certain ways of thinking may also suppress alternatives before they even receive a proper evaluation. This suppression may not even be intentional, but merely reinforced implicitly by hiring trends, for example. Young philosophers attempting to secure an academic appointment will be obliged to consider how they will be perceived as candidates by various hiring committees, and they will position themselves accordingly by means of the philosophical work they present. If the current recruitment trend is to hire those who are part of some dominant movement, then candidates will inevitably align themselves to that movement, else they risk not being hired and not being able to continue within the field of philosophy.[5]

Where the publication of philosophical views is controlled by editors who may be strongly constrained by certain philosophical traditions, alternative approaches may not even become widely available for consideration. An editor may simply reject those approaches by appealing to the standards of philosophical quality of the journal or the academic press, where those alleged standards may simply mask philosophical biases. Peer review processes do not mitigate this editorial suppression either, if editors request peer reviews of submissions only from those who share the philosophical biases of the editors.

Worse still, if a particular school of philosophy has an explicit political angle, such as Marxism, socialism, or conservatism, then

---

[5]In this context, I think of the one-way rivalry between Schopenhauer and Hegel, which was certainly made worse by Schopenhauer's attitude and actions, for example, insisting on teaching at the same time that Hegel lectured (Cartwright, 2010, p. 363). Where the trend at the time was to follow Hegel, how could Schopenhauer expect to remain part of the academic philosophical establishment without following Hegel to some extent? The case of Schopenhauer would seem to be a cautionary tale for young philosophers intent on running counter to the current philosophical trends, but a dubious one.

the institutions that support those philosophical schools may in fact function as extensions of associated political parties. The demarcation between partisanship in philosophy and political partisanship can easily be obscured, where think tanks aligned with political parties commission studies by philosophers, for example, or politically motivated individuals sponsor prizes for works of philosophy supporting their positions, or special interest groups apply pressure to universities to challenge academic freedom around the expression of certain views.

The extent to which any of these forms of partisanship actually occurs may indeed be questioned, but it is certainly not beyond question that some such partisanship does occur. The position taken in this book is that a difference across sides of an issue is not problematic in itself, but constitutes part of a healthy democracy, though it does become problematic when organizations in the form of political parties form around such sides, and those parties are supported by a network of other organizations and institutions. The same pattern of criticism applies equally to partisanship in philosophy, where differences in opinion across sides of a philosophical question are essential for the continuing development of philosophy, but organizations and institutions explicitly aligned to one side of certain philosophical questions tend to corrupt philosophy.

Chapter 8

Natural Slavery and Partisanship

Let me be clear at the start: I do not intend to condone slavery in any form here. Rather, my linkage of slavery with partisanship in the context of this book should clearly demonstrate that I am against both. However, I have always thought that Aristotle's notion of natural slavery had an element of truth that was not appreciated by those who self-righteously condemn slavery in any form and thereby condemn by reflex any arguments that do not similarly condemn slavery as stridently as possible. There is no imputation of condoning slavery by virtue of recognizing natural slavery, any more than the claim that some people are naturally stupid condones stupidity, though both claims might be incorrect. Indeed, I am not claiming that anyone is or was a natural slave. I am merely interested in the idea of natural slavery and its connection with partisanship.

In the United States it is nearly impossible to have a rational conversation about Aristotle on natural slavery, given the history of African slavery in the country and its continuing impacts. Of course, for Aristotle, slavery was a risk that any person might face, regardless of one's race. An invading army might subdue one's city-state and enslave everyone, including kings and philosophers. Yet Aristotle does seem to have some prejudices concerning natural slavery, but not against Africans specifically, rather against anyone who was not Greek. The only people he specifically accuses of natural slavery are "Asiatics" (Aristotle, 1984, p. 2039 [1285a20]), by which he seems to have meant Persians.

Aristotle makes a distinction between natural slavery and slavery by convention, where "The convention is a sort of agreement — the convention by which whatever is taken in war is supposed to belong to the victors" (Aristotle, 1984, p. 1991 [1255a6–7]). He introduces this distinction to account for the difference in opinion between those who claim that "slavery is both expedient and right" (Aristotle, 1984, p. 1991 [1255a2]) and those hold that slavery is wrong, where the latter are apparently thinking of slavery by convention, not natural slavery, in Aristotle's view. Yet Aristotle himself does not clearly and explicitly acknowledge that slavery by convention is wrong, only that the convention in question cannot by itself represent justice if the war by which people were enslaved was unjust (Aristotle, 1984, p. 1991 [1255a24–25]), and that war should not be pursued in order to enslave "those who do not deserve to enslaved" (Aristotle, 1984, p. 2116 [1333b39]). That appears to be as far as he argues against slavery by convention.

With regard to natural slavery, though, Aristotle is clear that precisely because some people are slaves by nature, this is both expedient and right. Yet his argument for natural slavery is strained and unpersuasive. The argument is fundamentally analogical in nature, on analogy with the soul and the body, whereby it is the soul that commands and the body that obeys (Aristotle, 1984, p. 1990 [1254a34–35]). He claims that slaves have no deliberative faculty (Aristotle, 1984, p. 1999 [1260a12–13]), in which case indeed it would seem that such slaves would need someone to provide direction. However, that would mean strictly that only the most mentally defective people would qualify as natural slaves according to this criterion, and it would seem that the vast majority of the slaves Aristotle had known and possible owned were not natural slaves at all. Perhaps Aristotle simply was not interested in the deliberative capabilities of the slaves of which he was aware. More importantly, just because people who are considered mentally defective in some way might need direction, that does not thereby mean that such a person should be treated as "a living possession" (Aristotle, 1984, p. 1989 [1253b32]).

Aristotle also notes that "where the relation of master and slave between them is natural, they are friends and have a common interest" (Aristotle, 1984, p. 1992 [1255b13]). Ross points out that the attribution of friendship here contradicts what Aristotle claims elsewhere, that as a slave, the slave cannot be friends with the master (Aristotle, 1984, p. 1835 [1161b5]) (D. Ross, 1995, p. 251). As people, though, the slave and master may be friends; yet such a relationship between people indicates that the kind of slavery in question cannot be natural slavery, but must be slavery by convention, else it seems that there would be no basis for friendship between a rational master and a mentally defective natural slave. Nor can one treat the fact of a common interest between master and slave as a criterion or even an indicator for natural slavery, since free people may obviously have common interests among them without the question of natural slavery arising, and a slave by convention may recognize that it is merely expedient to adopt a common interest with the master, at least temporarily.

Consequently, it seems that Aristotle's arguments for natural slavery do not succeed, but rather simply reflect the slaveholding prejudices that Aristotle shared with much of the ancient world.

Yet there is one characterization of natural slavery in Aristotle that suggests to me that the notion of natural slavery is not completely null and void. Aristotle claims, "For he who can be, and therefore is, another's, and he who participates in reason enough to apprehend, but not to have, is a slave by nature" (Aristotle, 1984, p. 1990 [1254b21–22]). Here Aristotle is emphasizing the lower faculties of reason allegedly held by the slave, as part of his strained analogy between soul and body. However, if one puts Aristotle's intention aside and focuses on the notion of "one who can be another's" then I think that a more viable sense of natural slavery emerges.

Suppose that someone is captured into slavery as a consequence of war and is told that he is now the property of someone else. Most people would rebel at the notion of being someone else's property, even if it is expedient to submit temporarily to the imposed slavery in order to preserve one's life. Suppose however that the person in question is perfectly satisfied to be the property of someone, relieved no longer to be obliged to make decisions for himself, content simply to do what he is told. Suppose that on the death of the slave-owner, the slave's first question is not "Will I be freed?" but "Who shall own me now?" In this case, it would indeed seem that the person was a natural slave in a sense, a willing slave, precisely because the idea of being a slave felt perfectly natural to him.

Still, in this case, it is not clear that it is fully natural for the person in question to think himself a natural slave, since this tendency may have been imposed by conditioning. If one has been born into slavery and has not been given the opportunity even to consider that one might not be a slave, then it is false to impute that attitude to any natural state. The attitude would have been forced on the person, whereas being raised in different circumstances would have led to a different attitude.[1]

Furthermore, it is not clear whether anyone would qualify as a natural slave even according to this conception. It may simply represent a distinction in principle rather than a distinction in fact, precisely because *no one* happens to react to the imposition of slavery in this way. At least one hopes that no one is such a natural slave.

However, if one puts aside the aspect of natural slavery whereby one is explicitly the property of someone else, there is still a question whether there are people who are perfectly satisfied to have someone else tell them what to do and how to act, rather than being obliged to determine this for themselves. Likewise, there is a question whether there are people who are perfectly satisfied to have someone else tell them how to think and what to believe. It is not clear to me that there are *not* such people, though I would wish there were not.

Of course, if one grows up in a particular tradition or culture, then there may be quite a lot that is prescribed for one to do and to believe in order to remain in that tradition. Yet there is a difference between having *some* things prescribed to one and wanting to have *most* things dictated.

Étienne de la Boétie was puzzled why people would put themselves in voluntary servitude to a petty tyrant, even when they have superior numbers and sufficient force to overthrow him (de la Boétie, 1975, pp. 48 ff), a point likewise recognized by Hume (Hume, 1987, pp. 32 ff). Custom and the favors that a tyrant bestows explain this voluntary servitude to some degree (de la Boétie, 1975, pp. 64–65, 69–71); however, de la Boétie claims that "the essential reason why men take orders willingly is that they are born serfs and are reared as such" (de la Boétie, 1975, p. 67). This is

---

[1] Compare Rousseau: "If there are slaves by nature, it is because there have been slaves against nature. Force made the first slaves, and their cowardice perpetuated the condition" (Rousseau, 1993, p. 183).

where I think there is some truth to the idea of natural slavery.

In the book on technology, I describe the difference between authenticity and inauthenticity in terms of one's level of alignment to the groups in which one finds oneself. Where one tends to accept every value that the group values, to endorse every decision that the group makes, and to participate in every action that the group takes, regardless of whatever group one finds oneself a member, that constitutes inauthenticity, since the person is not authentically an individual person, but is merely a reflection of the rest of the group. This seems to constitute a kind of natural slavery, where one is content to do what others tell one to do or to believe what others tell one to believe. The difference in this case seems to be that one is a slave to a group or even to an abstraction, rather than to another person, so it does not obviously feel like one has enslaved oneself. Yet the patterns are the same, with similar impacts.

Political parties tend to depend on natural slavery in this sense of inauthenticity, since they cannot effectively coordinate votes or other actions if there is authentic disagreement among their members or adherents. Once the party determines that it will take a certain position on an issue, then it wants its followers simply to adopt that position uncritically, encouraging them to believe that the position is right because that is what a good party member should believe. A more insidious case would be one in which the adherents to a particular political party uncritically accept the party line thinking that such is what they naturally believe, without acknowledging that they have given themselves in mental slavery to the political party and are willing and even eager to accept whatever the party claims they should do or think.

Such is the pattern of partisanship in general, whether political, religious, or even philosophical. One is a natural slave to a particular party if one *can* enslave oneself to the party line, whether deliberately or otherwise. Not every partisan is a natural slave in this sense, but it may be that every natural slave inevitably becomes a partisan.

Chapter 9

Allegedly Wasted Votes

In the transition to a state without political parties, anti-partisan candidates for political office will need to compete against candidates who are still aligned to political parties. On such occasions, it is inevitable that partisan candidates will try to argue to voters that voting for a candidate not aligned to a political party will only waste one's vote.

Gary W. Cox claims that "it does not take a rocket scientist to understand traditional wasted vote arguments" (Cox, 1997, p. 89). Likewise, Duverger refers to the notion of a wasted vote as though it were clear and uncontroversial (Duverger, 1964, pp. 226, 248, 323), as does Lijphart (Lijphart, 1994, p. 97). Yet Michael Dummett claims that the notion of a wasted vote is muddled (Dummett, 1997, p. 120), and Robert D. Behn and James W. Vaupel argue that there is a fallacy in appeals to wasting one's vote (Behn & Vaupel, 1984). Perhaps, then, the alleged understanding of wasted vote arguments to which Cox refers may be faulty, and some measure of intellect comparable to that of a rocket scientist should be expended in examining the notion of a wasted vote and arguments against wasting one's vote.

The notion of a wasted vote is often invoked within the context of discussions of proportional representation, which is usually advocated as a way to avoid wasting votes, since the proportionality of representation is derived from all votes — except, however, for electoral systems in which there is a threshold of votes that must be met in order to have offices allocated proportionally. Voting for a party that does not meet such a threshold would apparently still waste those votes.

Yet if the notion of a wasted vote is invoked as a factor in the choice of one electoral system over another, such as the decision to adopt a system of proportional representation rather than some other electoral system, Dummett claims that there ought to be a general conception of a wasted vote that could be applied in such a choice, rather than a notion of a wasted vote relative to a particular electoral system. Dummett considers a pair of proposed definitions of a wasted vote, and finds them both faulty, which confirms Dummett's assessment that the notion is simply muddled:

1. "one has wasted one's vote, under any particular electoral system, if, by voting differently, one could, *under that same system*, have obtained an outcome one preferred" (Dummett, 1997, p. 111)

2. "for the voters in a given set to be said to have wasted their votes, [it must be the case] that, if they had voted differently, they could have made *certain* of getting an outcome that they preferred, however the other electors voted" (Dummett, 1997, pp. 111–112)

Dummett does seem sympathetic to the application of the first definition within a plurality electoral system, particularly in a three candidate contest, in which a voter's preferred candidate finishes third, while a candidate that the voter detested wins, since if the voter had voted for the candidate who finished second, the detested candidate might not have won. Yet ultimately, Dummett even questions the value of that notion of a wasted vote:

> But, when wasted votes are under discussion, it is necessary to ask what makes wasting one's vote a bad thing. If, under the plurality system, an elector realizes that, if he had voted differently, he might have helped a candidate that he preferred to win, he will regret the way he voted. But, given the candidate who did win, the fact that he did not contribute to his victory is no *additional* cause of regret; and, if he could have done nothing to prevent that victory, he will have no regrets about the way he voted. (Dummett, 1997, p. 117)

These considerations are supported by Behn and Vaupel, who examine two cases in a three party election for office, in which a voter has a strong dislike for one candidate, designated *Disaster*, a strongly favorable opinion for another, designated *Allworthy*, and indifferent feelings toward the third, designated *Lackluster*. The two scenarios correspond to whether or not Allworthy has a chance to win the election, and in both scenarios they argue that the voter should still vote for Allworthy in most cases. They conclude, "Unless your distaste for candidate Disaster is very great and his race with Lackluster is so extremely close that your support could be decisive, the real waste is to support Lackluster rather than Allworthy" (Behn & Vaupel, 1984, p. 612).

In a plurality election in which there are more than two candidates, it seems clear to me that all appeals to wasted votes are simply attempts at coercion. Suppose that one of the two leading candidates claims that voters are wasting their votes if they do vote for a candidate who does not have a chance to win, meaning one of the two leading candidates. If those voters accept this argument and consequently vote for that candidate's opponent, the candidate's argument will have undermined that candidate's campaign. Consequently, that candidate will only make the argument to voters whose second choice is that candidate. To voters whose second choice is the candidate's opponent, that candidate will be happy to have those voters waste their votes, rather than to give the candidate's opponent additional votes. Consequently, in such a case, the notion of a wasted vote is relative to the candidate making the claim, and the ultimate meaning of the notion is the dubious claim that any vote not cast for the candidate making the claim is wasted since it does not thereby contribute to that candidate's election. From the perspective of an individual voter, that vote does not seem to be wasted at all, so long as it reflect's the voter's actual preference, as Dummett suggests and as Behn and Vaupel demonstrate.

Under an electoral system in which voters rank candidates in order of their preference, such as the systems of Alternative Vote or Single Transferrable vote, Dummett notes that "a different meaning [is conferred] on 'wasting one's vote'", namely that "The only wasted votes will be those which were never transferred to a candidate who was eventually elected" (Dummett, 1997, p. 117). Within such systems, and according to this meaning of a wasted vote, any appeals to wasting one's vote can thereby be equated to an attempt at coercion as well, since a candidate or an advocate for a candidate making such an appeal is essentially attempting to get voters to vote in the most favorable way toward that candidate by means of the preferences the voters indicate on their ballots, since the argument is unlikely to be made at all if the allegedly wasted vote is cast favorably to the candidate making the argument according to some level of preference.

Under a system of proportional representation, however, a vote for a party typically does contribute to the number of seats that the party is allocated in the legislature, at least in aggregate, and therefore the vote is not wasted within the logic of this system unless it is cast for a party that fails to meet an initial threshold. Yet the price for the avoidance of allegedly wasted votes under this system is the acceptance of political parties, which the main argument of this book in Part I has found to be unacceptable.

Consequently, I suspect that relative to any given electoral system the notion of a wasted vote is problematic, whether because the notion is ultimately an attempt at coercion on the part of candidates to gain more votes or because it contributes to the continuation of political parties.

Therefore, following Dummett's line of argumentation, there is a two-part argument against the notion of wasting one's vote:

1. There is no valid notion of wasting one's vote independent of particular electoral systems, as Dummett has argued.

2. Relative to a particular electoral system, any conception of wasting one's vote either amounts to coercion on the part of candidates to gain more votes or supports an electoral system that entrenches political parties.

Any unsuccessful candidate for office will have wasted resources and energy in a campaign that did not attain its goal, and political parties will certainly seek to minimize such waste. Accordingly, votes themselves may come to be considered political resources that may be expended well or poorly, and perhaps this notion of waste may have become conflated with a waste of a vote from the voter's own perspective. Yet one's vote is not fundamentally a resource to be expended in order to further someone else's political goals. Rather it is an expression of one's political preferences within the range of alternatives presented at an election. The election itself represents an aggregation of interests represented by these political preferences across the entire electorate, rather than considering political parties to function as a aggregation of interests, as discussed in Section 3.6.

If none of the alternatives on a ballot represents one's interests, then leaving one's ballot blank does not represent a waste of one's vote either. It represents precisely the best approximation of one's political preferences, namely that the desired alternative simply does not appear on the ballot. Casting one's ballot for a candidate that does not properly represent one's political preferences seems to be a greater waste, since the opportunity is lost for expressing dissatisfaction with the available political alternatives, and the candidate who received the vote will mistakenly interpret that vote as full endorsement of the candidate's policies or character, which is not the case. Thus I claim that a proper democracy should ensure that every ballot includes an option indicating "none of the above" allowing voters to express dissatisfaction with all available candidates, and that such votes should be explicitly tallied and reported.

For those not sufficiently motivated even to go to the polls to cast a ballot, their apathy constitutes a null vote not only against every candidate on the ballot, but also against the entire democratic process. There seems to be no better or more efficient way to express the political position of such potential voters.

Consequently, I claim that no vote is wasted unless it is coerced against one's genuine political preferences, even a vote that is not even cast.

Chapter 10

The Irrelevance of Ideology

I can imagine a wide range of people endorsing the idea of the abolition of political parties, so long as their own political party is exempted: "Certainly other political parties ought to be abolished because they are fundamentally wrong. My political party, however, is correct and therefore should be preserved."

Accordingly, one might challenge the main argument of this book by observing that it does not take into account what particular political parties stand for. Whatever the faults of political parties in general may be, if there is a political party that endorses a set of policies that is beneficial for a nation or a community and has the political power to implement those policies, it seems that it would be wrong to advocate the abolition of that political party.[1] The key questions thus would seem to be what are the ideologies of particular political parties and whether those ideologies are beneficial or not, regardless of what adverse impacts may or may not be associated with the structure of the political party that espouses that ideology.

It should not be surprising to learn that I have no affection for ideologies, given the line of argumentation in Part I. A set of beliefs that is posited as a single unit that one is expected to endorse altogether seems to represent the essence of political inauthenticity. Even if I happen to endorse every belief contained within the ideology, I do so not because the belief is packaged as part of an

---

[1] However, as I have argued in Section 2.3, the chance that a given political party represents all the policies that happen to be optimal for a nation or community is extremely low.

ideology, but because each belief has merit on its own. Authenticity requires one to evaluate each belief independently, not simply to accept them because they are part of an ideology.

One problem with ideologies is that it is often difficult to understand all of the beliefs that are associated with a given ideology at any given point in time. It is not the case that an ideology constitutes an explicitly formulated set of beliefs, such as a catechism or articles of faith, despite the intentions of Destutt de Tracy, who coined the term 'ideology' to represent a science of ideas (Destutt de Tracy, 1804, pp. 4–5). Rather, an ideology in practice is a vague set of beliefs or even tendencies that may change over time. It is fundamentally an abstraction, rather than a concrete set of beliefs. Some beliefs may be explicitly articulated as part of an ideology, particularly core beliefs, but the vagueness of an ideology is partly due to the consequences that might be drawn from those core beliefs, which require a measure of interpretation, thus introducing indeterminacy into the ideology. Such indeterminacy allows an unscrupulous advocate of an ideology to insert potentially problematic beliefs into the ideology, claiming that they are consequences of the core beliefs of the ideology, whereas they may only follow based on highly strained interpretations of those core beliefs, or may rest on unstated presuppositions. For those accustomed or even conditioned to align themselves mentally to follow some ideology, this indeterminacy provides an opportunity to be manipulated.[2]

Political parties will typically pose their current policies in the form of an intrinsic ideology to which adherence is demanded in the interest of party unity. Even if the party espouses openness among its members or adherents, the ideology operative in a party will inevitably need to be enforced, since a fundamental reason for having a political party is to enact definite policies by collective action, not to provide a forum for debate on what those policies might be.

Yet my main argument here is not that these aspects of the ideologies associated with political parties support the call for the abolition of political parties. Any such considerations were already inherent the arguments in Chapter 2. Rather, the argument is that

---

[2] Geertz likens ideology to metaphor, in a positive sense of its adaptability to changing political situations (Geertz, 1973, p. 220), but such adaptability can also have negative consequences, as suggested here.

the question of particular ideologies and their merit as well as the problems inherent in ideologies are irrelevant to the question of the abolition of political parties. The preceding remarks strongly indicate that those who reject ideologies in general, as I do, should support the abolition of political parties. I will argue further that those who do accept ideologies in general and support a particular ideology should likewise reject political parties, with the consequence that political parties should be abolished whether one endorses or rejects ideologies.

If I do support some ideology, it is not always clear that there will be a political party that is already aligned to that ideology at any given time, although I may certainly start such a political party, assuming that there are others that likewise support the same ideology.[3] Of course, it may happen that I support an ideology specifically because I have committed myself to the political party and that I inauthentically adopt whatever party line the political party says that I should adopt. Yet such considerations were already part of the argument in Chapter 2.

Suppose, however, that there is an ideology that represents all of my beliefs, including the full consequences of those beliefs according to an interpretation that I support. Suppose further that there is a political party that endorses that ideology in its entirety. The problem is that the political party is not likely to continue to endorse that ideology, at least according to my preferred interpretation of that ideology.

Ideologies embodied within a political party at a given time are often formed in contradistinction to policies espoused by competing political parties, particularly in party systems dominated by two major parties, as in the United States. If one political party proposes some policy, then since the other political party is in opposition to that party, the opposing party is likely to oppose the policy in turn, primarily to ensure that no political ground is conceded to the party that proposed the policy.[4] In this way, the ideology of

---

[3] However, Michels provides an interesting quotation from Rodbertus noting that leaving a political party to start a political party provides no guarantees that same problems in the old party will not recur in the new one (Michels, 1915, p. 387). Where the problems in question represent a failure to adhere to some ideology, this observation is relevant to the line of argument that follows here.

[4] Hofstadter quotes Fisher Ames in 1800 speculating that dread of a rival holds a party together (Hofstadter, 1969, p. 145).

a political party may shift over time, not in accordance with any fixed guiding principles of the party, but according to the vagaries of political expediency.[5] If the ideology of the political party shifts in this way, and my ideology has not, then the political party no longer supports my ideology. Since this can be true for any political party, even for a political party that I explicitly start in order to support my ideology, I cannot trust political parties to champion my ideology.[6]

Therefore whether one accepts ideologies or rejects them, ideology becomes essentially irrelevant. In neither case is the argument for preserving political parties strengthened, so ideology can be ignored as a factor, leaving the arguments against political parties in Chapter 2 unaffected.

---

[5] (Sinhababu, 2016) claims that it is coalition politics that unifies parties, not ideologies.

[6] Mannheim suggests that this is a failing of those who adopt a fixed ideology, or a fixed vision of a utopia as well, which represents a "distorted mental structure" (Mannheim, 1960, p. 87), where reality is actually more dynamic (Mannheim, 1960, pp. 84–87). Yet the reality to which Mannheim refers seems itself to be problematic and perspectival precisely under the influence of ideology and utopia (Mannheim, 1960, pp. 87–96).

Chapter 11

Democracy According to Follett

In the first decades of the twentieth century, politics in the United States was encumbered not only with political parties, but also by political machines such as Tammany Hall. Yet Mary Parker Follett spent no time arguing that these organizations should be abolished. Rather, she bluntly asserts that one key mistake with regard to direct government is "in thinking that we can get any benefit from it if it is operated from within the party organization" (Follett, 1918, p. 177). "'Representative government,' party organization, majority rule, with all their excrescences, are dead-wood" (Follett, 1918, p. 4). Her focus is thus primarily on what should succeed political parties and their associated mechanisms: "In their stead must appear the organization of non-partisan groups for the begetting, the bringing into being, of common ideas, a common purpose and a collective will" (Follett, 1918, p. 4).

Follett pointedly claims, "We talk about the evils of democracy. We have not yet tried democracy. Party or 'interests' govern us with some fiction of the 'consent of the governed' which we say means democracy. We have not even a conception of what democracy means" (Follett, 1918, p. 3). She proceeds to articulate a new conception of democracy, whereby "Democracy is the rule of an interacting, interpenetrating whole" (Follett, 1918, p. 156).

The basis for Follett's conception of democracy is the proper interaction of groups in contrast to crowds, where "the crowd and the group represent entirely different modes of association"

(Follett, 1918, p. 85). The operative notion of a group for Follett thus emerges from a series of contrasts:

group "I have used group in this book with the meaning of men associating under the law of interpenetration as opposed to the law of the crowd — suggestion and imitation" (Follett, 1918, pp. 22–23).

crowd "Crowd action is the outcome of agreement based on concurrence of emotion rather than of thought, or if on the latter, then on a concurrence produced by becoming aware of similarities, not by a slow and gradual creating of unity" (Follett, 1918, p. 85).

mob "The laws of the mass as of the mob are, it is true, the laws of suggestion and imitation, but the mob is such an extreme case of the mass that it is necessary to make some distinction between them. Emotion in the crowd as in the mob is intensified by the consciousness that others are sharing it, but the mob is this crowd emotion carried to an extreme. As normal suggestibility is the law of the mass, so abnormal suggestibility is the law of the mob" (Follett, 1918, p. 88).

herd "The satisfaction of the gregarious instinct must not be confused with the emotion of the crowd or the true sense of oneness in the group. ... The 'comfort' of feeling ourselves in the herd has been given as the counterpart of spiritual communion, but are we seeking the 'comfort' of fellowship or the creative agonies of fellowship. The latter we find not in herd life, but in group life" (Follett, 1918, p. 89).

numbers as mere numbers "When we are a lot of people with different purposes we are simply wearied, not stimulated. At a bazaar, for instance, far from feeling satisfaction in your fellow-creatures, you often loathe them. Here you are not swayed by one emotion, as in a crowd, nor unified by some intermingling of thought as in a group" (Follett, 1918, p. 89).

Yet Follett is careful not to propose these contrasts as though they represented clear distinctions. "It is often difficult to determine whether a number of people met together are a crowd or a group (that is, a true society)" (Follett, 1918, p. 87). "We must not, however, think from these distinctions that man as member of a group and man as member of a crowd, as one of a herd or of a mob or of a mere assemblage, is subject to entirely different laws which never mingle; there are all the various shadings and minglings of these which we see in such varied associations as business corporation, family, committee, political meeting, trade-union etc." (Follett, 1918, p. 90).

Thus it is the group process, not crowd interactions, that will be the basis of Follett's conception of democracy. She describes this process in terms of the paradigm of committee interaction in contrast to voting on pre-conceived ideas. "I go to a committee meeting in order that all together we may create a group idea, an idea which will be better than any one of our ideas alone, moreover which will be better than all of our ideas added together. For this group idea will not be produced by any process of addition, but by the interpenetration of us all" (Follett, 1918, p. 24).

For example, if A, B, and C are members of a committee, it is not the case that ideas from B and C are added to some initial idea from A to produce some group idea.

> They will not add any more than apples and chairs will add. But we gradually find that our problem can be solved, not indeed by mechanical aggregation, but by the subtle process of the intermingling of all the different ideas of the group. A says something. Thereupon a thought arises in B's mind. Is it B's idea or A's? Neither. It is a mingling of the two. We find that A's idea, after having been presented to B and returned to A, has become slightly, or largely, different from what it was originally. In like manner it is affected by C and so on. But in the same way B's idea has been affected by all the others, and not only does A's idea feel the modifying influence of each of the others, but A's ideas are affected by B's relation to all the others, and A's plus B's are affected by all the others individually and collectively, and so on and on until the common idea springs into being. (Follett, 1918, pp. 24–25)

Given this process for creating a collective will, in contrast to a conception of a pre-existing general will as Rousseau seems to have assumed (Follett, 1918, pp. 48–49),[1] Follett proceeds to propose a restructuring of democratic society starting with neighborhood organizations that enact decisions using this group process (Follett, 1918, pp. 189 ff), citing the success of such cooperative neighborhood organizations in the First World War (Follett, 1918, p. 237, note 1). With these ground-level neighborhood organizations in place, governance at the level of a city would be assembled on the basis of representatives from neighborhood organizations, and similarly at progressively higher levels, thus providing democratic integration of each level of government: "The neighborhood must be actually, not theoretically, an integral part of city, of state, of nation" (Follett, 1918, p. 246). Each group of representatives at the level of a city, state, and nation would likewise employ Follett's group process to create a collective will, thus implementing Follett's conception of democracy.[2]

The experience of the United States in the First World War gives Follett encouragement to think that her recommendations for democratic changes to the structure of governance will work. The Council on National Defense implemented local councils at the levels of states, counties, and even communities, primarily to facilitate the flow of wartime information from the national level down to small communities. Follett thinks that such organizations can facilitate not only the flow of information from the top down, but also to ensure that decision-making proceeds from the bottom up. "If ...the country wishes to be really a democracy, the neighborhood groups must have a share in forming the aims and the policy," prompting Follett to ask rhetorically, "why should we be more efficiently organized for war than for peace?" (Follett, 1918, p. 248).

Besides this integration of government from neighborhoods to progressively larger groups, Follett also sees a place for representation of occupational groups in government, so long as these groups do not dominate, since occupational groups can only represent part of a whole person (Follett, 1918, pp. 291 ff). However, Follett is not perfectly clear how neighborhood groups and occupational groups would function together in a large democracy, merely not-

---

[1] See Chapter 12 for my reflections on one conception of the general will, which I believe survives Follett's criticism that "Many people talk as if the collective will were lying around loose to be caught up whenever we like" (Follett, 1918, p. 48).

[2] For a similar proposal, see (Stickney, 1890).

ing that "We may perhaps come to wish for an integration of neighborhood and industrial groups — and other groups too as their importance and usefulness demand — as their 'objective' value appears" (Follett, 1918, p. 320).

There is much that is compelling about Follett's conception of democracy, given the integration of government from local to state to national levels. In particular, congenial to the argument in Part I of this book, Follett claims:

> An effective neighborhood organization will deal the death blow to party: (1) by substituting a real unity for the pseudo unity of party, by creating a genuine public opinion, a true will of the people, (2) by evolving genuine leaders instead of bosses, (3) by putting a responsible government in the place of the irresponsible party. (Follett, 1918, p. 217)

Indeed, Follett identifies a set of problematic reasons for the acceptance of political parties:

- "The party has dominated us in the past chiefly because we have truly believed the people to be a crowd" (Follett, 1918, p. 181).

- "We have accepted party dictatorship rather than anarchy. We have felt that any discussion of party organization was largely doctrinaire because party has given us collective action of a kind, and what has been offered in its place was a scattered and irresponsible, and therefore weak and ineffective, particularism" (Follett, 1918, p. 218).

- "Men follow party dictates not because of any worship of party but simply because they have not yet any will of their own. Until they have, they will be used and manipulated and artificially stimulated by those who can command sufficient money to engage leaders for that purpose. Hypnosis will be our normal state until we are roused to claim our own creative power" (Follett, 1918, p. 221).

I will not contradict any of these assertions.

Yet there are many aspects of Follett's proposals that I think are problematic:

1. Follett herself poses one problem: "We do not yet know, for instance, the best number to bring out the group idea, the number, that is, which will bring out as many differences as possible and yet form a whole or group. We cannot guess at it but only get it through scientific experiments. Much laboratory work has to be done" (Follett, 1918, p. 30). Yet if this number is not known, how can Follett expect that a neighborhood organization will be able to generate any collective will, rather than merely degenerating into unproductive argumentation? Perhaps a neighborhood is too large, in which case a smaller group would be needed, thus requiring an additional layer of government to enable effective group deliberations. However, more layers of government would thereby pose additional problems of integration, and it is not clear that Follett's proposals would be sufficient to provide unity across an expanding hierarchy of government.

2. The notion of neighborhood groups makes sense in an urban or suburban context, but what constitutes a neighborhood in rural areas, particularly where one's closest neighbor may be miles away? Although rural areas are now much less isolated than when Follett wrote, such that it is at least possible for rural people to meet together more easily, it is still less convenient for rural groups to meet together than it is in an urban neighborhood. Furthermore, the awareness of common issues may not be as clear in rural areas. While there are some issues that do require coordination among rural neighbors, even at a considerable distance, such issues may not have the same urgency or immediacy as in a dense urban neighborhood, where a water main break, for example, may impact everyone in the neighborhood.

3. Follett proposes that neighborhood groups send representatives to deliberate in groups at the city or county level. Those representatives would clearly be chosen among members of the neighborhood by those same members, so the selection of a representative for the neighborhood would constitute a form of direct democracy. However, city or county groups would likewise send representatives to deliberate at the state or provincial level, and those representatives would be chosen by and from among members of the city or county

groups, not by all the citizens of the city or county that they represent, and likewise for representation at the national level. It is not clear that the representatives chosen by intermediate and higher groups would reflect the preferences of citizens of the entire district had the choice been offered to them in an open ballot. This indirection of representation may result in a government that is increasingly disconnected from individual citizens, rather than constituting a greater level of integration.

Since representatives at the national level are selected from representatives at the state or provincial level, who are selected from representatives at the city or county level, who in turn are selected from members of neighborhood groups, Follett argues that this arrangement is designed precisely to ensure that government at higher levels remains connected and integrated with lower levels, including neighborhood groups that are directly responsive to individual citizens whom those groups comprise. Yet the consequence would seem to be that representatives at a national level should have duties also within those groups at the state or province, city or county, and neighborhood levels. It would be difficult or even impossible for a single representative to devote sufficient time to deliberations within each of these groups.

Perhaps at best representatives would be fully engaged in the group at the highest level of representation to which they have been selected, while periodically reporting back to the group at the next lower level. Therefore, there would be ample opportunity for a disconnection at higher levels of representation from individual citizens, such that it is not clear how such a hierarchy of representation would constitute a more integrated democracy than in cases where representatives are directly selected from and by members of the entire constituency they represent.

4. Follett makes a curious admission that she has in the past rejected prospective members from inclusion in committees she was organizing, either because they were inclined to give advice or merely to observe, rather than to participate in the kind of group process she advocates (Follett, 1918,

p. 29). Yet such individuals ought to be members of some neighborhood organization according to the new structures of democracy that Follett advocates. Does Follett plan on excluding these citizens from her democracy? Apparently so, since she claims, "We all need not merely opportunities to exercise democracy, but opportunity for a training in democracy. We are not going to take any kind of citizen for the new state, we intend to grow our own citizens" (Follett, 1918, p. 207), devoting an entire appendix to "The Training for the New Democracy" (Follett, 1918, pp. 363 ff). The consequence seems to be that the new democracy will begin not as a democracy at all, but a broad aristocracy of those who are willing and able to merge themselves into the group process, until those who cannot do so will die off and a new generation of citizens is raised with the training to participate in Follett's conception of democracy. Yet can a democracy worthy of the name begin that way?

5. In the book on technology, I discuss the notion of inauthenticity formulated by philosophers such as Kierkegaard, Nietzsche, and Heidegger as immersion in some abstractions such as *the public, the herd*, or more generally *they* (Ressler, 2024, pp. 85 ff). Follett's distinctions among groups, crowds, mobs, and herds suggest that she is sensitive to the forces of these abstractions, even if she does not reference Kierkegaard or Nietzsche, whom she may have had an opportunity to read, unlike Heidegger who published after she wrote. By advocating for groups over crowds or herds, she seems to be advocating for authentic group interaction rather than inauthenticity. Yet from the distinctions Follett makes among these kinds of aggregates, it is not clear to me that the mechanisms for achieving a collective will are any different from the forces of inauthenticity.

Follett notes that she has been accused of mysticism in advocating for group processes among individuals (Follett, 1918, p. 6) or even nations (Follett, 1918, p. 346). In response, she claims that her proposal simply represents sensible psychology. Yet the psychology of groups tends toward conformity to the group, in a manner perfectly consistent with inauthenticity, such that the reason group ideas emerge in the way that Follett advocates is precisely because those ideas are grounded in patterns of inauthenticity, not because individuals authentically engage in group deliberations.

6. To expand upon the previous point, Follett wrote decades before Irving Janis articulated his Groupthink hypothesis, according to which there is "a mode of thinking that people engage in when they are deeply involved in a cohesive in-group, when the members' strivings for unanimity override their motivation to realistically appraise alternative courses of action" (Janis, 1982, p. 9). The group process that Follett describes seems highly susceptible to Groupthink, such that a collective will may indeed be identified from the group process, but such a will may be faulty in its consequences, even disastrous.

Janis gives recommendations for avoiding Groupthink, starting with the following:

> The leader of a policy-forming group should assign the role of critical evaluator to each member, encouraging the group to give high priority to airing objections and doubts. This practice needs to be reinforced by the leader's acceptance of criticism of his or her own judgments in order to discourage the members from soft-pedaling their disagreements. (Janis, 1982, p. 262)

While this recommendation is not logically incompatible with the kind of group deliberations that Follett advocates, it does require a strong measure of individuality, which Follett clearly discourages. Throughout her presentation, Follett consistently subordinates individuality to group identity, as evidenced by statements such as:

- "We find the true man only through group organization. The potentialities of the individual remain potentialities until they are released by group life. Man discovers his true nature, gains his true freedom only through the group" (Follett, 1918, p. 6).

- "...there is no such thing as an individual conscience in the sense in which the term is often used" (Follett, 1918, p. 55).
- "But the individual is not for a moment to yield his right to judge for himself; he can judge better for himself if he joins with others in evolving a synthesized judgment" (Follett, 1918, p. 55).
- "If my true self is the group-self, then my only rights are those which membership in a group gives me" (Follett, 1918, p. 137).
- "Individual competition must, of course, disappear. All must see that the test of success is ability to work with others, not to surpass others" (Follett, 1918, p. 364).

Yet the peculiar form of individuality that Follett finds in the group is precisely what contributes to the patterns of Groupthink that Janis identifies, prompting Janis to advocate that each member of the group explicitly takes the role of critical evaluator. To adopt this role is to step away from any collective will, at least temporarily, in order to see where the collective will might be faulty, and this stepping away entails that risk that one may thereby no longer be willing to conform to the direction the rest of the group is taking.[3]

Consequently, if Janis is correct, the group process is not sufficient to enable an effective democracy, but democracy also requires a strong measure of individuality and authenticity in the contrary direction to ensure that Groupthink is not mistaken to represent a collective will. Nor does the group process encourage the kind of authenticity that is necessary among individuals. Yet were such authenticity achieved broadly among individuals, it is not clear that Follett's recommendations are strictly necessary to achieve a genuine democracy. Rather, it seems that a vital form of democracy could develop within the current system of electoral representation among citizens who are politically authentic.

---

[3] Janis's presentation emphasizes the role of a leader whom those in the group are trying to please, such as a President. However, the same patterns of Groupthink may emerge when an abstraction takes the place of a leader, such as the abstraction of an ideology or of party spirit, even as a neighborhood.

Therefore the issue is not the structures of democracy, as Follett claims, but the inauthenticity of citizens.

Given such problems, democracy according to Follett may represent an unattainable ideal, an ideal that might be achieved if citizens were more broadly authentic in their political choices. However, if citizens were more authentic in this way, then they may see democracy and the political structures needed to realize it differently than Follett does. While Follett describes some deliberative qualities and conditions that may be desirable in representatives to a legislature, as described similarly in Section 5.2, those conditions may not be required at all levels of society according to the structures that Follett recommends.

The priority, then, would be to remove the obstacles to democracy first, then to allow political structures and institutions to adjust and to develop accordingly as citizens become increasingly more authentic in their political thinking. The argument in Part I suggests that it is political parties that are the greatest obstacles to democracy. Once political parties are abolished, perhaps Follett's conception of democracy may be realized, but it is more likely that something quite different may emerge. If we take Follett's own remarks against experts seriously (Follett, 1924, pp. 3–30), then it should be the citizens, as a group, that decide what structures of democracy should evolve, not experts like Follett herself.

Chapter 12

General Will, not Necessarily According to Rousseau

Although I aim to be a careful reader, I occasionally misread some writers, sometimes disastrously, but sometimes profitably. It seems that for many years, I may have been misreading Rousseau on his conception of the general will. Perhaps so. All the better, then, since I can thereby claim the misconception of the general will as my own conception, with Rousseau merely serving as an occasion for its formulation.

Yet I do not consider Rousseau to have delineated his conception of the general will exceptionally well, such that my misreading should be considered inexcusable.[1] The one concrete example of the exercise of the general will that I have found in *The Social Contract* is in the establishment of a dictatorship, which will be discussed below, and which seems highly problematic.

Likewise problematic is the following description of what Rousseau apparently considers to be a paradigm case of the exercise of the general will:

> When, among the happiest people in the world, bands of peasants are seen regulating affairs of State under

---

[1] Others concur. For example, Ostrogorski finds numerous inconsistencies in Rousseau's presentation of the general will (Ostrogorski, 1902b, pp. 674–676). Wolff claims that his notion is simply ambiguous (Wolff, 1970, p. 57).

an oak, and always acting wisely, can we help scorning the ingenious methods of other nations, which make themselves illustrious and wretched with so much art and mystery? (Rousseau, 1993, p. 271)

In this instance, it seems that a general will is being brought into existence by a process of negotiation, not that there is a pre-existing general will that merely comes to light by discussing issues beneath an oak tree.[2] Negotiations can proceed in different ways, depending upon the skills of the various negotiators, so the emergence of a consensus in such cases may simply reflect the persuasiveness of certain parties, rather than representing a common good for the community that would have been realized even if those persuasive parties had not been present.

The following are the characteristics of the general will that I can identify within Rousseau's presentation:

- The general will is relative to a particular group of people.

  In discussing an aristocracy, Rousseau identifies two corporate bodies, the aristocracy and all of the citizens, and therefore two general wills corresponding to them (Rousseau, 1993, p. 238). In this case, those in the aristocracy are also part of the corporate body that they govern, yet the general will of the entire corporate body does not simply apply to the subset of that corporate body, which has a will of its own. Presumably also the general will of the subset of the entire corporate body without the aristocracy would likewise constitute a separate general will than that of the larger corporate body in its entirety.

- Associations and factions are contrary to the general will of the entire corporate body.

  This seems to follow directly from the previous characteristic, since if a subset of the corporate body may have a different general will than that of the entire corporate body, then associations and factions will count as such subsets and therefore have different general wills aligned to each of them. Rousseau explicitly points out this consequence, particularly

---

[2]See Follett's criticisms of Rousseau's general will (Follett, 1918, p. 48), also referenced in Chapter 11.

noting the destructive effects if one of those factions overwhelms the others (Rousseau, 1993, pp. 202–203). Political parties certainly count as associations that are contrary to the general will, and therefore this aspect of Rousseau's presentation of the general will is congenial to the arguments in this book; however, note that my arguments in Section 2.3 do not depend in any way upon a notion of the general will, whether according to Rousseau's conception or my apparent misreading of Rousseau, which will be described below.

- The general will is an aggregation of particular wills of members of the corporate body, in some way evening out the differences of those particular wills.

Rousseau offers a hazy mathematical description, contrasting the "will of all" with the general will, whereby "the latter considers only the common interest, while the former takes private interest into account, and is no more than a sum of particular wills: but take away from these same wills the pluses and minuses that cancel one another, and the general will remains as the sum of the differences" (Rousseau, 1993, p. 202). Shortly after this passage, he likewise refers to the general will as "a sum of small differences" (Rousseau, 1993, p. 203). In some way, the pluses and minuses of these small differences remove private interests and leave only common interest, though the exact calculus seems somewhat mysterious. Note that this calculus cannot result in what is in the interest of people most generally, since in that case there would seem to be no difference between the general will of an entire corporate body and the general will of a mere faction, for whom the common interests of people in general would still apply. Therefore, there must be some particularity remaining that is characteristic of one group of people that is not identical with a subset of that group or even a different group of people.

- The general will must be general in its content, not merely shared generally across the entire corporate body.

As Rousseau says, the general will "must both come from all and apply to all" (Rousseau, 1993, p. 204), and therefore it "cannot pronounce on a man or a fact" (Rousseau, 1993,

p. 205), by which he clearly means that it cannot pronounce *only* on a particular person or a particular case. By virtue of applying to all, the general will thereby will pronounce on every particular person or case that falls under the scope of the general will, but in the same way in which it applies to all others.

- Voting among the corporate body is indicative of the general will, but only imperfectly so.

Although Rousseau claims that "what makes the will general is less the number of voters than the common interest uniting them" (Rousseau, 1993, p. 205), the notion of voting or at least deliberation seems important to the notion of the general will. "To be general, a will need not always be unanimous; but every vote must be counted" (Rousseau, 1993, p. 200, footnote). Indeed, "counting votes and comparing opinions" appears to be the primary means by which the general will may be discovered (Rousseau, 1993, p. 274), though the methods for doing so can vary. Further, Rousseau considers voting to be an inalienable right of citizens (Rousseau, 1993, pp. 272–273). Yet he acknowledges a presupposition that "all the qualities of the general will still reside in the majority" going further to suggest that it possible for this not to hold, in which case "liberty is no longer possible" (Rousseau, 1993, p. 275). This is a significant presupposition that makes appeals to the general will problematic in every practical instance, if voting cannot always determine the general will.

- There are apparently priorities that can be identified within the contents of the general will.

This characteristic appears to follow from Rousseau's curious endorsement of dictatorships in certain circumstances, claiming that even the suspension of a legislature in favor of a dictatorship is consistent with the general will: "In such a case, there is no doubt about the general will, and it is clear that the people's first intention is that the State shall not perish" (Rousseau, 1993, pp. 290–291). Yet in such an instance, it is likely that the people's second intention, whatever that may be, will not necessarily be upheld in the establishment of a dictatorship. Consequently, the general will appears to allow for priorities in which not all of the general will may be upheld at all times, so long as the top priorities that are willed are upheld. It is not clear whether the preservation of the State is the sole aspect of the general will that may be prioritized above all others for Rousseau, or whether every aspect of the general will may be ordered in priorities. The will to establish a dictatorship appears to be the one concrete example of the general will that Rousseau provides, and I find it highly problematic.

After researching the idea of authenticity in Kierkegaard, Nietzsche, and Heidegger in the book on technology (Ressler, 2024), what strikes me especially strongly on re-reading Rousseau is how closely his notion of the general will seems to align to the abstractions that foster inauthenticity, such as Kierkegaard's *the public*, Nietzsche's *herd*, and Heidegger's *they*. The calculus of cancelling out pluses and minuses that Rousseau describes in the establishment of the general will seems to align precisely with the process of leveling that Kierkegaard describes. Of course, Rousseau claims repeatedly that the general will is focused on common interests among the corporate body, but he does not actually prove this. Perhaps it is a mere hope on Rousseau's part that summing the allegedly small differences in determining the general will leaves only common interests in the remainder, but given the analysis of inauthenticity beginning with Kierkegaard, it seems characteristic of *the public* that *they* will claim that the leveling and censoring that *they* impose are for the common good, whether that is true or not. Rather, perhaps Rousseau is himself the dupe of an abstraction he calls *the general will*, fostering inauthenticity as the foundation for the authority of a state that pretends to represent the will of all those who submit to its authority precisely by virtue of leveling off any will that runs counter to it, and indeed in its inauthenticity by creating conditions under which any will that is contrary to it tends not even to arise. Since the idea of authenticity was articulated after Rousseau's death, it is not perfectly clear how Rousseau might react to such an accusation. It seems that he ought to be embarrassed by it; however, for my part, I am not completely certain that he would be.

The characteristics of the general will outlined above do not themselves constitute an interpretation of the general will. Rather, they represent conditions taken directly from Rousseau's text that ought to apply to every adequate interpretation.[3] As I noted above, I am not convinced on re-reading the text that my interpretation of Rousseau's general will is adequate.[4] However, if I am right that Rousseau is ultimately relying on forces of inauthenticity to justify his social contract, then I will be pleased that my interpretation does not align well with Rousseau. In that case, I prefer my faulty interpretation to whatever Rousseau may actually have thought.

My interpretation starts with Rousseau's claim that the general will "must be general in its object as well as its essence" (Rousseau, 1993, p. 204), namely that the generality in the general will is found not only in its manifestation across the general population, but also in the generality of its content. Rousseau explicitly claims that this means that the general will "cannot pronounce on a man or a fact" (Rousseau, 1993, p. 205); yet I interpret this condition more strongly. Where Rousseau speaks of summing the pluses and minuses, I interpret him to be referring to the abstraction away from particular content in individual wills in order to establish generality.

For example, suppose that people in a community want to create a park. People in the north part of the community want it established at a particular location in the north, whereas people in the east, south, and west want it located at different sites closer to them, according to their place of residence. Focusing on the particular wills, it seems that there are four different factions, each with their own general wills to create a park at one of four different locations. However, if the specifics of *where* the park is located are abstracted away from these particular wills, then a common general will can indeed be identified, namely that a park be created somewhere within the community. Consequently, wherever the

---

[3]Weil claims that there are two conditions for the general will (Weil, 2014, pp. 8–10), but these are conditions for the application of the general will, rather than conditions for an adequate interpretation.

[4]Nor am I convinced that other interpretations of Rousseau's general will meet the conditions that I have identified in his text, particularly those relying on some counterfactual, such as "The general will, then, may be what people would want if they knew enough" (R. G. Ross, 1953, p. 112), which seems a typical example of this kind of interpretation. How does this interpretation account for the relativity of the general will? How does this interpretation represent an aggregation of pluses and minuses from particular wills?

park is eventually created, the general will would appear to be satisfied, though many particular wills are not. Only if the park fails to be created at all, perhaps precisely due to the disagreement over where to create it, does the general will fail to be satisfied. It seems that such generality might be established across a wide range of contrary particular wills by abstracting away specifics of *who*, *what*, *where*, *when*, and perhaps even *why* and *how*.

That last form of abtraction is particularly interesting, though perhaps problematic. Perhaps everyone in a community may agree that something needs to be done, that some particular result needs to be effected, but there may be considerable disagreement on *how* that result is to be accomplished. In that case, whatever means are adopted to accomplish the result, it would appear that the general will is satisfied — so long as those means actually do accomplish the result. Yet what if they do not? Then it seems that the decision to adopt the means was not in accordance with the general will after all. Consequently, this case would seem to differ from the example about creating a park where the adoption of any of the particular wills appeared to accomplish the general will. The correct choice of *how* to accomplish the result is a key part in determining whether the general will is actually served or not. In this case, it seems that no calculus of summing the pluses and minuses, which I have equated to the forces of leveling in inauthenticity, will serve to determine the correct course of action to take. It may require expertise to determine *how* to accomplish the desired result, and that expertise tends to be among the exceptional elements that get leveled off by the forces of inauthenticity. Of course, it could still be maintained that the general will was clear in its remaining content, though not with regard to the proper means to achieve that general will.

Yet if the general will is insufficient to determine the best means to accomplish the general will, then why should I be confident that the general will represents the common interest, as Rousseau repeatedly claims that it does? Rousseau asserts that the common will does not require unanimity (Rousseau, 1993, p. 200, footnote), but unanimity if it does occur apparently establishes a common will (Rousseau, 1993, p. 273). The problem is that the common will may not recognize the unforeseen consequences of certain decisions, which may only be appreciated by a very small minority, whose votes get canceled out in the summing of pluses and minuses. It may even be the case that *no one* in the community recognizes these unforeseen consequences, in which case the general will under this interpretation would not represent the best interests of the community. In an early draft, Rousseau recognizes a distinction between "apparent interests" and "interests properly understood" (Rousseau, 1993, p. 177), but nothing in Rousseau's presentation of the general will guarantees that it will secure the proper interests of a community. This Rousseau acknowledges when he considers the question "Whether the general will is fallible" (Rousseau, 1993, p. 202), but he lays the blame on associations and factions, as noted above in the characteristics of the general will. In the end, Rousseau naively relies on the precautions of proliferating factions to ensure that none become predominant as "the only ones that can guarantee that the general will shall always be enlightened, and that the people shall in no way deceive itself" (Rousseau, 1993, p. 203). There simply is no such guarantee, since no one has perfect insight into the consequences of any decision, particularly if the most insightful members of the community are leveled down to the level of the average. The only way that the kind of generality that Rousseau seems to advocate could be infallible is by generalizing to the point of vacuity, namely that the general will is for the proper interests of the community to be realized, whether or not anyone in the community knows what those interests actually are.

Of course, these considerations are based on my own interpretation of Rousseau, and therefore if they lead to problematic conclusions for Rousseau, that would seem to indicate mainly that my interpretation of Rousseau was faulty according to the principle of interpretive charity. Yet I have not heard another interpretation that does not rely on some mystical ability for the members of a community to identify their own best interests, while adhering to the characteristics of the general will that I have identified above from Rousseau's text. Perhaps there is no such interpretation, and the fault lies in Rousseau.

I still prefer my interpretation of the general will, even if it is not sufficiently charitable toward Rousseau. My interpretation is not strong enough to justify the authority of the state, but that was never my goal — quite the opposite, since this book emerged from questions whether organizations such as political parties are needed at all, and a subsequent question to ask is whether even states are needed. The reason I consider the question of Rousseau's general will at all, besides the repeated references to it in many of the sources cited, is that my apparently faulty interpretation of Rousseau seems suggestive in considering how responsible legislators could function productively in a democracy without political parties, as described in Chapter 5. For this purpose, I do not need a notion of general will at all, whether infallible or not, so long as legislators are capable of considering contrary demands from multiple constituents in a way that is conducive to some resolution that does not simply decide in favor of some at the expense of others. Seeking to generalize in the way proposed in my interpretation of the general will seems to be at least one way for legislators to proceed. I suspect that there are others that will be discovered, once political parties are abolished, and the habits of reliance on and complicity with their partisanship is eradicated.

Chapter 13

Rights and Responsibilities

I must have read suggestions concerning the connection between rights and responsibilities numerous times, but it never made a strong impression on me until recently. For example, on re-reading Rousseau's *Social Contract* in writing Chapter 12, I encountered the following statement: "It is no good your telling me that by renouncing the duties which natural law imposes on me I at the same time deprive myself of its rights, and that my violent actions will authorize all those which anyone may wish to commit against me" (Rousseau, 1993, p. 173). I most certainly read this passage in college, again in graduate school, and a third time in preparation for teaching a course. However, the link between rights and responsibilities on which this passage depends never seemed to register in my consciousness. Furthermore, this is merely one reference, and I cannot imagine how many other times I have encountered this connection in other books, simply because the notion did not seem important enough to me.

By a connection between rights and responsibilities I do not mean the usual sense in which my rights entail other people's responsibilities to honor those rights.[1] I mean that rights granted to me entail responsibilities on my part.

Mary Ann Glendon argues that the impoverished quality of discourse concerning rights in the United States has suppressed considerations of responsibilities and sociality, even discussions of these factors (Glendon, 1991). So indeed, this may account for why

---

[1] As schematized by Hohfeld in his set of jural opposites and correlatives in (Hohfeld, 1913, 1917).

I previously failed to appreciate the connection between rights and responsibilities, however much I may pride myself on my ability to recognize the value of ideas that I encounter in books, even very obscure ones.

Having finally come to recognize this connection between rights and responsibilities, I consider it to be the single most important political principle. Glendon seems to allow that there may be some rights that are not linked to any responsibilities when she refers to "... the responsibilities, if any, that should be correlative with a given right; ... " (Glendon, 1991, p. 177), but I think the connection between rights and responsibilities is stronger: No rights without correlative responsibilities; no responsibilities without compensatory rights.

In fact, I hypothesize that the connection between rights and responsibilities is at the heart of the notion of justice. Suppose that one person in a community has far greater rights than others, but with no additional responsibilities, or perhaps with no responsibilities at all. Conversely, suppose that someone has much greater responsibilities than others, but no additional rights. These seem to be clear instances of injustice. One might try to claim that the issue is not injustice in such cases, but rather simply inequality. Yet it seems impossible that every community can impose the same responsibilities on each of its members, because not all of those members are equally capable of fulfilling those responsibilities. A form of equity is achieved in balancing the difference in responsibilities with a correlative differences in rights, and it is this kind of equity that I claim forms the fundamental principle of justice.

Note that the metaphor of a balancing scales has traditionally been associated with justice, at least back to ancient Egyptian times. Of course, philosophical analysis cannot rely primarily upon a metaphor, but nor can it simply ignore metaphors that have been so prominent for so long. The balancing within this metaphor is traditionally interpreted as a weighing both the accusation and defense of an accused person, but I suggest that it should more properly represent the balancing of rights and responsibilities.

I have never been completely comfortable with the term 're-tributive justice' that links the notion of retribution to justice, and the term 'rectificatory justice' does little better, by focusing primarily on a wrong and how to make it right. Certainly if someone has been wronged by someone else, the injured party should receive some measure of compensation if justice is to be served, but this restrictive conception of justice does not fully represent the justice that needs to be served on the part of the wrongdoer. If, however, justice is understood in terms of a balance between rights and responsibilities, then that balance will already have been set by a community, whereby the wrongdoer had a responsibility that was not upheld, in which case that wrongdoer should expect that certain correlative rights would need to be forfeited as a consequence, whether the right to retain a certain amount of property, the right to liberty for a certain period of time, or even the right to life if the failure of responsibility is serious enough according to the standards of the community. This characterization of justice seems to be more complete than merely invoking retribution or rectification.

Nor do I think that distributive justice requires a significantly different analysis than what has traditionally been called retributive justice. I have been dubious of the notion of 'global distributive justice' since I first heard the term. I have come to suspect that the problem with this notion is somewhat similar to Kant's presentation of the Transcendental Dialectic, whereby certain questions become undecidable because reason extends inferences beyond all possible experience (Kant, 1965, pp. 297 ff). Indeed, if someone bakes a pie that is to be shared among a group, one might raise the question of justice regarding how portions of that pie are distributed. However, it is not clear that such questions can properly be raised globally. Firstly, it is not clear that everything ought to be distributed globally at all, and many discussions of global distributive justice do not consider the question of how much ought to be distributed and how much should not be subject to any distribution at all. Secondly, just because goods are in fact allocated to people, organizations, and other entities, in which a global distribution can be recognized at any given point in time, that does not mean that there must be a distribution principle to which the notion of justice must be applied. Nozick clearly saw this (Nozick, 1974).

However, I consider both Nozick and Rawls to be inadequate in their competing analyses of justice. The problem that I suspect is that Nozick over-emphasizes rights where Rawls over-emphasizes responsibilities (Rawls, 1999), and the reverse. An adequate analysis of distributive justice, more properly understood broadly as economic justice, would ground it fundamentally in the balance between rights and responsibilities, as with any form of justice, in my judgment.[2]

I would begin such an analysis with the notion of property, which traditionally gets analyzed primarily in terms of the rights of the property owner, often with provisions for the revocation of such rights in retribution or recompense for some offense on the part of the property owner. By contrast, I have come to think that any property primarily entails significant responsibilities, and that any rights associated with the holding and the use of that property must be concomitant with the proper execution of those responsibilities.

For example, with regard to land that is treated as the property of someone, that land typically hosts a variety of living creatures, whether animals, insects, plants, and even microbial life. It therefore seems to me that any owner of that land considered as property has some responsibility to the life on it. Note that this responsibility does not entail a commitment to the absolute preservation of any right to life on the part of the living creatures on the land. Nature itself does not work this way, and the imposition of any right to life universally on the natural world would be disastrous, since life feeds on life. Yet nor can the property owner properly and ethically dispose of that life however the owner pleases, despite what prevailing laws may claim.[3]

Furthermore, I think that even property in the form of artifacts likewise entails certain responsibilities. Any material artifact embodies a certain amount of resources, both in the form of raw ma-

---

[2]Note that this diagnosis aligns with my methodological thinking to be presented in a forthcoming book tentatively entitled *Perspectival Methodology*, according to which the difference in perspectives on a given philosophical issue can profitably be employed as a methodological device. A perspectival analysis would identify the presuppositions underlying different perspectives and would analyze them into dimensions that become a critical part of the resulting analysis of the issue. Here the key dimensions are rights and responsibilities, where Nozick and Rawls each seem to presuppose an emphasis of one over the other in certain cases, and the resulting perspectival analysis would hold that justice constitutes a balance between them.

[3]Such considerations form part of the third projected book on ecology in this series of applied philosophy. Consequently, arguments for these bare assertions here will be deferred until they can be investigated in greater detail.

terials as well as the work of laborers and craftsmen.[4] I claim that responsibilities are owed regarding those resources. Even if it is claimed that I have the right to treat an artifact that I own in any manner that I please, even to destroy it wantonly if that is my wish, which is a claim that I do not accept, I still at least have a responsibility to dispose of the resulting waste properly. I do not have a right to leave the waste in my neighbor's lawn or in the middle of a public street, for example.

Consequently, I think that all forms of justice are ultimately founded upon the connection between rights and responsibilities, whereby justice consists of a proper balance between them. How to achieve this balance may not be clear in any given case, and the particular patterns of balance achieved by one community may not be applicable to another community, but these seem to pose practical problems not conceptual ones. This conception of justice supports a wide range of alternatives for people within a society to determine the kind of lives they want to lead within the bounds of justice. Any community will impose a minimal set of responsibilities on all of its members as a condition for remaining within the community, and some communities may impose a very high level of responsibilities. So long as the community grants correlative rights for the responsibilities it imposes, justice is maintained. However, the range of possibilities available within a given society can constitute a measure for the freedom of that society. If I want to minimize my responsibilities, can I renounce the compensatory rights associated with them, perhaps by owning as little property as possible? If I want more rights, do I have the opportunity to undertake additional responsibilities? There will be limits in any society, but societies that offer wider ranges for just balances between rights and responsibilities seem thereby to have higher levels of freedom.

Yet I did not invoke the notion of a connection between rights and responsibilities here primarily to discuss the conception of justice, which requires much greater analysis and argumentation to support the bare assertions presented here. As suggested in footnotes in the book on technology (Ressler, 2024, pp. 60, 62), the connection between rights and responsibilities provides a basis for

---

[4] See, for example, the place of artifacts in the structural analysis of technology presented in (Ressler, 2024, p. 31).

a useful principle in understanding the difference between organizations and mere groups. If there are no rights or responsibilities associated specifically with regard to the group, but any relevant rights and responsibilities ultimately devolve onto the individual members of the group, then that group seems quite different from an organization. If rights are granted specifically to the organization separate from the rights held by members serving in roles within the organization, then it should be expected that additional responsibilities will be demanded from that organization correlative to those rights.

Thus, the difference between the groups on the left and right sides of Table 1.1 in the Introduction can be understood in terms of the relationship between rights and responsibilities with regard to the group and its members. In a side or even a faction, there are no rights associated to the group as such, and therefore no responsibilities expected of it. Any rights or responsibilities in question must be aligned to the individual members of the group. However, political parties are granted rights, such as the right to raise funds held by the party, and the right to have their candidates listed under party labels on election ballots. Even with regard to a caucus within an organization, that organization may grant rights to the caucus as a whole, such as the right to present an issue collectively as a caucus, or the right to meet within facilities maintained by the broader organization. In these cases, though, it may be difficult to identify the responsibilities corresponding to these rights, and that might part of the problem with these organizations.

It is this aspect of organizations in general that make them problematic, in the way that political parties have been argued to be problematic in Part I. Even if explicit responsibilities are assigned to organizations, perhaps by law, the organization in question cannot accept those responsibilities in the same way that an individual person accepts responsibilities, namely that the entire person accepts the responsibility. In an organization, it is typically one or more persons acting within certain roles that are responsible for meeting the responsibilities of the organization as a whole. Some organizations may indeed train its members to consider that each of them is responsible for meeting the organization's collective responsibilities; however, it is still the case that certain roles have responsibilities associated with them that are not applicable to other roles. All members of an organization may indeed have the responsibility not to violate the applicable laws of the society in which the organization operates, and indeed an individual organization member may personally be held accountable by that society for violations, but if the member was acting in a particular role within that organization, the organization as a whole is also held accountable. For other issues, though, the member of the organization may be held personally accountable only to the organization, and may be dismissed from the role held within the organization, with the organization as a whole held accountable for what was done on its behalf by someone acting within a role.

The problem is precisely in the fragmentation of persons into roles and in the corresponding potential for inauthenticity of people acting within those roles, as argued in the book on technology.[5] Where one can simply say, "I was just serving a role, just following the organization," the level of personal responsibility gets diminished, with the consequence that the responsibilities expected of the organization as a whole get compromised. In these cases, the corresponding kinds of organizations become problematic, and therefore it seems that they should be subject to greater scrutiny. If the structure of organizations of a particular type consistently compromises the satisfaction of the responsibilities that should be expected from those organizations, then it seems that their corresponding rights should be challenged. Stronger still, perhaps they simply should not be allowed to exist and should be abolished.

---

[5] Particularly in (Ressler, 2024, Chapter 3).

Chapter 14

Anarchism and the Value of Unattainable Ideals

Previously I have argued that organizations such as political parties are one of the key factors compromising an authentic engagement with technology, and indeed compromising authenticity in general (Ressler, 2024). In this book, I argue that political parties are unnecessary and indeed problematic for democracy and that they should be abolished, as previously advocated by Simone Weil. A natural question that follows is what other organizations might likewise be abolished, such as companies, corporations, states, and nations. Perhaps those who have advocated so passionately for anarchism have been correct.[1]

Thoreau writes:

> I heartily accept the motto, — "That government is best which governs least"; and I should like to see it acted up to more rapidly and systematically. Carried out, it finally amounts to this, which also I believe, — "That government is best which governs not at all'; and when men are prepared for it, that will be the best kind of government which they will have." (Thoreau, 2001, p. 203)

For my part, I agree with Thoreau on both counts, but with one addition: I do not think that people will *ever* be prepared for a government that does not govern at all, or for the abolition of states

---

[1] See (Marshall, 2010) for a history of anarchist thought.

and nations in some anarchist future. If people in democratic societies so willingly continue to elect ineffective and irresponsive governments, aligned to problematic political parties that compromise authentic political engagement, then it seems improbable that they will ever be prepared on their own for anarchist self-government. Perhaps the poor governments that people currently elect are precisely what they are prepared for and precisely what people deserve if they cannot themselves see democratic alternatives. The best that can be hoped, it seems to me, is to convince people to abolish the political parties that perpetuate the current system of poor choices and to establish mechanisms that can provide better choices for electing more effective and responsive governments. If I am correct in this, then it would appear that anarchism is merely an impossible ideal. Rather than advocating an anarchist ideal that cannot ever be realized, it would seem more responsible to identify what balance between governance and freedom could realistically be attained, and to work toward that balance.

In the book on relativism, I discuss the possibility that even if an argument was self-refuting, it might be uroboric, invoking the image of a serpent swallowing its own tail, in that its self-refutation may intentionally be invoked to advance a particular position that might not have been attained without the self-refutation (Ressler, 2013, pp. 275–276). While anarchism is not commonly taken to be self-refuting, there may be something similar operative in anarchism such that even if it is clearly unattainable, the articulation of anarchist principles will not have been a wasted endeavor, and may achieve a secondary aim that was not attainable without having been framed in terms of anarchism.

Suppose then that anarchism is impossible. It may likewise be impossible to determine precisely what the proper balance between freedom and governance should be. Perhaps that balance is different for different sets of people. Perhaps that balance changes over time as circumstances change. Without the articulation of the impossible ideal of anarchism, the target level of balance may be set too low, and people may be convinced to settle for a higher level of governance than is strictly needed, thereby failing to achieve as much freedom as they could have attained. Whereas if the target is set higher than the actual balance should be, it is more likely that the proper balance could be attained, where government institutions and other organizations will always provide forces counter to freedom to ensure that the balance is not set too high toward freedom. By retaining the impossible ideal of anarchism, which by hypothesis sets the balance too high toward freedom, and by working to achieve as much of the ideal as possible, the target would never be set too low.

This seems to be the function of ideals in general, namely to set a target to which planning and action can be directed to achieve some desired state. Where that desired state is possible, and the target is attainable, the ideal represents the basis of a practical measure of what still needs to be accomplished to achieve that desired state. However, where that desired state is impossible, the ideal represents a persistent upward force that serves to achieve some optimal balance short of the desired state, where that balance may not be attainable without setting the target impossibly high.

Of course, I may be wrong in thinking that people will never be prepared for anarchism, or perhaps Thoreau and I are both wrong in thinking that people must be prepared for anarchism before they can have that allegedly best kind of government. Perhaps anarchism is attainable, and perhaps it can be attained without people being yet prepared for it, and people can be encouraged or obliged to adapt to it before they are fully ready. Without the ideal of anarchism at all, it is doubtful that people will simply find themselves suddenly emerging into a state of complete anarchist freedom without taking deliberate and intentional measures to realize that state, particularly given the contrary impacts of organizations such as political parties and existing government institutions.

Nor is it merely utopian political ideals such as anarchism that have this value, even if they are impossible. Suppose that dogmatic skeptics are correct and that knowledge is impossible. It does not follow from that supposition that the ideal of knowledge should thereby be abolished and that epistemology should substitute some lesser notion as the maximal cognitive ideal that can be attained. Knowledge still should remain as an ideal, even if an impossible ideal, pushing people to seek higher and higher levels of justification to the extent that is possible, where a lower ideal may be set too low, thereby compromising the benefits of various epistemic virtues. Consequently, it may be that Pyrrhonian skepticism is the best approach after all, whereby it is not known whether knowledge is possible or not, so long as the skeptics in question continue searching, as Sextus Empiricus claims they should (Sextus Empiricus, 2000, p. 3).

I think that scientific realism functions as another such ideal, whether attainable or impossible. Where fallibilism is part of any claim of scientific realism, the implication seems to be that scientific theories may not represent mind-independent truths about the world *yet*, and the appeal to some sloppy conception of *approximate truth* merely introduces metaphysical problems with regard to the nature of truth, without dispelling the suspicion that scientific realism is primarily an ideal to which science tends, as in Peirce's pragmatism. I think Hendry's arguments for methodological realism as "the claim that some practices that are central to the success of science reveal realist commitments" (Hendry, 1995, p. 54) captures the way in which this ideal actually functions. It is difficult to see how a practicing scientist could successfully work in a field such as particle physics, for example, without taking elementary particles and the laws governing them to be features of the world rather than as psychological or sociological constructs, else that scientist might end up performing a phenomenological analysis on particles as they appear to the scientist's consciousness rather than conducting physical experiments and gathering data. Yet whether what is said about elementary particles properly represents what the world is really like or not is not strictly established by virtue of scientific practice, however instrumentally successful those statements may be.[2]

With regard to the possibility of abolishing all organizations that compromise authenticity, including corporations and governments, I can therefore endorse anarchism, but only as a methodological ideal. I offer this book as evidence that one form of such organizations can be abolished, namely political parties. Other forms of organizations require additional investigation, analysis, and imagination to determine whether they too can be abolished, and I suspect that this additional work will be much harder than in the case of political parties. Yet this work will be prematurely compromised if the ideal of anarchism is not engaged fully, even if that

---

[2]In fact, I think that particle physics is most ready for a Kuhnian scientific revolution than any other scientific field. I suspect that the continuing impact of the particle metaphor has been compromising the formation of better conceptions of fundamental physics that might have better claim to represent reality.

ideal is in fact impossible.

Furthermore, if it is turns out that the abolition of political parties itself represents an impossible ideal that cannot practically be realized, contrary to my arguments, that would not thereby indicate that the arguments in this book were completely futile, for example, if the threat of effective abolition resulted in more responsible political parties. That mere possibility, though, does not undermine my commitment to the abolition of political parties. I stand by my arguments. Let the practical possibility or impossibility actually be demonstrated.

Chapter 15

Organizing Without Organizations

Typically people are acknowledged to have the right to organize themselves to take political action, and the resulting pattern of organizing is typically acknowledged to constitute an organization, therefore the arguments offered in this book against political parties, grounded in their status as organizations, may seem to undermine fundamental political rights of people.

Yet such an objection relies on equivocation on the term 'organization'. A pattern of coordination among a group of people to accomplish a goal does not necessarily constitute an entity called an organization separate from that group of people, unless one has explicitly been formed, for example by registering articles of incorporation with a relevant government institution. The right to organize for political action strictly entails the right to coordination, not necessarily the right to incorporation, though a nation might also grant that additional right. Further, effective political action may require coordination, but it does not clearly require the incorporation of an organization, whether formally or informally.

What this book and the book on technology have found important about organizations as separate entities above the groups of people that compose them at any time is the roles into which organizations structure people. Organizations characteristically have provisions for filling roles when prior occupants of those roles cease to occupy them, whether through dismissal, resignation, death, or otherwise. These provisions ensure that the organization as a whole continues to function potentially for an indefinite period of time, long after the original members of the organization have died. This characteristic indicates that the organization constitutes a separate entity in addition to the group of people associated with the organization, likewise indicated by the ability to have rights and responsibilities assigned to the organization that do not merely aggregate the pre-existing rights and responsibilities of the people occupying roles in the organization, as discussed in Chapter 13.

By contrast, coordination for political action need not rely on any fixed roles, but might focus rather on the specific activities that need to be performed in order to accomplish a goal. Those who may perform those activities today need not perform those same activities tomorrow, but may perform other activities.

Yet at a certain level of participation, the coordination between all participants may become so cumbersome that it may seem that an organization is required to manage the complexity. When the size of the group becomes too large simply to seek volunteers to perform certain activities, and the amount of activity increases beyond the ability of all members of the group to track it all, it seems that some individuals need to assume designated roles to specialize on certain functions. While it may be possible to create a network of connected smaller groups in some cases, where the smaller groups can continue to function simply as flexible groups without falling into roles, the coordination between these groups seems to require specialization into roles, else there would fail to be any continuity and stability in the coordination from one encounter between groups to another. In such cases, the progression from organizing to organization seems inevitable, and the resulting organizations run the risk that the organization may become the end rather than the means, as described by Ostrogorski, Michels, and Weil, and discussed in Chapter 2.

Indeed, this progression from mere organizing to organization forms the basis for a defense of political parties and an objection against the abolition of them. According to the objection, political parties provide the basis for stability and continuity of political action, without which individual citizens would eventually lose interest and the social movement in question would merely degenerate and dissolve. Consequently, since significant social and political change requires stability in order to achieve long-term goals, political parties are necessary, and their abolition would compromise the ability for citizens to accomplish their political goals.[1]

There is some justice in these considerations, but ultimately their force is over-estimated with regard to political parties. In particular:

- The objection tends to imply that without political parties, social movements would simply fade away without achieving any action. Indeed, some groups of activists may disband without an organization to sustain them, but if the issue is important enough, then why would not new centers of activity continue to form in their place? Contrariwise, if the issue is held together solely by the force of an organization such as a political party, rather than a continuing conviction of the value of the issue, then perhaps the issue is not sufficiently important after all.

- Why must a single organization in the form of a political party serve as the center of political action? As suggested in Chapter 3 and particularly Section 3.7, it might be better if the various functions that political parties serve are distributed across different organizations and different kinds of organizations.

- Political parties exist to seek and to preserve power. If a social movement is embodied in a political party, and if the goals of that social movement are actually accomplished by the political party, that party will not simply disband itself, but will redirect its organization to other goals, by the sheer force of bureaucratic momentum. At that point, the political party becomes an end in itself for perpetuating political power, rather than serving as the means for specific social goals.

So indeed it seems that some measure of organization rather than mere organizing may be required for significant social change, in order properly to coordinate extensive activities and to sustain commitment. Yet once these organizations start transforming themselves into political parties, they risk becoming part

---

[1] For example, (Rosenblum, 2010, pp. 353–356), though Rosenblum attempts to redirect the focus to partisanship rather than political parties, and this section in particular seems to rely on some equivocation between them.

of the structure of political problems, rather than solutions. In particular, if a strong movement to abolish political parties emerges in some nation, perhaps as a result of the arguments within this book, it cannot properly form itself into a political party to achieve that goal. Further, if the movement forms into one or more organizations to coordinate political action, it must self-consciously and perpetually take measures to ensure that it does not become the very beast that it is trying to slay.

Chapter 16

On the Possibility of Taming Organizations

As noted in the Introduction, the same general strategy applied regarding the possible abolition of political parties could be employed in evaluating other kinds of organizations, namely:

- Evaluate whether the organizations cause definite harm to people.

- Determine whether the functions of those organizations can be served in other ways or whether those functions need to be served at all.

- Explore how people in various roles can continue to achieve their goals without those organizations.

If the organizations in question do not cause any harm to people, then there would seem to be no problem to be solved, particularly if the organizations provide some definite benefit.

If the organizations do cause harm, but the functions of that organization can be served in other ways such that people can achieve their goals without those organizations, then there would seem to be a clear case for abolishing that kind of organization.

The problematic case is where the organizations represent a necessary evil, namely that there is some definite harm caused by the organizations, but the beneficial functions served by the organizations cannot be served in other ways, such that the abolition of that kind of organization would also impose some harm on people.

Perhaps commercial corporations and nations fall into this category, though this will not be perfectly certain until evaluations are actually performed. In these cases, what is needed is some way to mitigate the actual and potential harms, namely a way to tame the organizations in question.

One might immediately think that regulations should be imposed as a way to control these harms, but regulations may not always be completely effective. The problem is that it may be possible to regulate against specific harms, but it is not always feasible to regulate the root cause of those harms. Thus some specific harms may indeed be controlled, but if the root cause remains in place, other harms will inevitably arise in their place.

With regard to political parties, there have been a few arguments attempting to mitigate their harms, including those of Ostrogorski, as discussed in Section 5.1. The author of *Federalist* Number 10 claims, "There are two methods of curing the mischiefs of faction: the one, by removing its causes; the other, by controlling its effects" (Hamilton et al., 1788, p. 54). The methods for removing the causes of faction seem unpalatable: "The one by destroying the liberty which is essential to its existence; the other, by giving to every citizen the same opinions, the same passions, and the same interests" (Hamilton et al., 1788, p. 54). The remaining option is to control the effects of faction, which the author argues is in the creation of the Federal government of the United States. Yet this option does not appear to have cured the mischiefs of faction after all.

Sidgwick discusses a number of measures for controlling the ill effects specifically of two-party government:

- Withdraw some legislative and administrative work from party control, in favor of committees;

- Retain knowledgeable individuals as heads of departments, rather than allowing such positions to become political spoils;

- Introduce a referendum;

- Improve the morality of the nation to put duty before party (Sidgwick, 1891, pp. 575–577).

Sidgwick adds, "And probably the country would gain from an increase in the number of persons taking a serious interest in politics who keep out of party ties altogether" (Sidgwick, 1891, pp. 577).

My argument is stronger, namely that political parties should be abolished entirely, and that the country would gain from an increase in political authenticity in the absence of political parties. Yet in the case of organizations besides political parties that cannot be abolished because they are necessary to some degree, measures for controlling their effects must be found. For specific kinds of organizations, some measures comparable to the ones that Sidgwick describes with regard to two-party government might be found, but the remainder of this chapter will briefly consider a key mitigation factor that might apply to organizations in general, assuming that they cannot simply be abolished.

The argument in the book on technology is that the nature of organizations tends to encourage inauthenticity, particularly among the members of the organization itself, but also those outside the organization, by reducing people to specific roles (Ressler, 2024, pp. 59–61). It may be that the harms attributed to certain organizations can be traced to this tendency toward inauthenticity, as it was in the case of political parties. If so, then the question is how to control this tendency toward inauthenticity.

As part of that previous argument, it was suggested that as more people working within an organization exhibit authenticity, the organization as a whole would tend to reduce the pressure toward inauthenticity that it exerts on people within and outside the organization (Ressler, 2024, pp. 106–107), where authenticity requires the following conditions:

1. One must be able to imagine alternatives.

2. One must prefer at least one of those alternatives.

3. One must have the courage to stand up for that alternative in the face of opposition.

4. One must persevere in the face of opposition. (Ressler, 2024, pp. 96–99)

Within an organization, these conditions would need to be applied to each decision that each person makes in each role that person serves. The crucial condition is the first one. If one continues to act merely in accordance with a role in the organization, then it is easy to fall in line with the standard alternatives that are already aligned to that role and to implement those alternatives, regardless of the potential for harm. Authenticity means that one does not merely act according a role, but acts as a whole person within that role, meaning that one acts as a person who serves multiple roles in different contexts, who has relationships both inside and outside the organization, relationships according to which one has a wide range of responsibilities. Acting authentically within a role in an organization entails that one recognizes alternatives that may align to a wider range of responsibilities than just the narrow range of responsibilities linked to that organization role, and presumably someone acting authentically would also prefer alternatives that accord with the widest range of these responsibilities, including broad moral and ethical responsibilities, needless to say.

Of course, there are limits to the courage and perseverance required for authenticity, if one finds that one is continually challenging the decisions that the rest of the organization makes. In that case, one might find oneself ejected from the organization. Yet if one is continually at odds with the direction of the rest of the members of an organization, then perhaps it would be best not to be part of that organization in that case. However, if all people who challenge the direction of the organization either resign or are ejected, then the organization will eventually consist only of those who think alike, in which case the chances of exhibiting authenticity within the organization would steadily decrease, thereby reinforcing the inauthenticity that was posited as the source of the evils that the organization inflicts, however necessary those evils may be. Consequently, it may be that an organization that refuses to countenance any significant measure of disagreement within its ranks is doomed to stagnate into inauthenticity, until and unless external pressures force a change.

Therefore, the question remains how to induce people within an organization toward authenticity in the first place.

Internal to the organization, it may happen that someone who already exhibits a degree of authenticity achieves a position of responsibility sufficient to encourage authenticity within the organization more broadly, but this would seem to be a rare case, particularly since an organization grounded in inauthenticity will tend to hire and to promote those who align to this pattern of inauthenticity, ejecting those who challenge this tendency too far.

External to the organization, it may be possible for authentic individuals to exert pressure on an inauthentic organization, in cases where that organization is subject to competitive forces, as in a commercial corporation, where such people would tend to prefer to patronize organizations exhibiting authenticity. Yet this too presupposes that there are enough authentic individuals outside the organization to make a difference, which merely shifts the question from how to induce people toward authenticity within the organization to how to induce authenticity in people outside the organization. If there were a sufficient number of authentic people outside the organization, then pressure would already be exerted in these cases, assuming that such people could gauge the levels of authenticity of competing organizations, perhaps measured in terms of the overall harms caused by those organizations.

Ultimately, whether inside or outside an organization, people will not demand authenticity if they are not aware of what it is and what are the consequences of inauthenticity. Consequently, it becomes a matter for education. However, educational institutions are themselves organizations that can exhibit varying levels of authenticity or inauthenticity. There are indeed educational institutions that do foster a strong sense of authenticity in students. It would seem that there are not enough. If there were, then it would seem that inauthenticity would not be such an issue.

Of course it is not clear that there are any organizations that count as necessary evils according to the supposition of this chapter. It may be that for any type of organization to which definite harms can be attributed, there are alternatives to the functions that these organizations serve such that that the evils are not necessary at all. These are points that will need to be demonstrated for specific types of organizations. If enough people continue questioning whether organizations are really necessary, though, it may be sufficient to keep such organizations adequately tamed in order to control their potential for harms. For example, if political parties were indeed abolished, other types of organizations would thereby be on notice. They might be next.

References

Aldrich, J. H. (2001). *Why parties? a second look.* Chicago & London: The University of Chicago Press.

Aristotle. (1984). *The complete works of Aristotle* (Vol. 2; J. Barnes, Ed.). Princeton: Princeton University Press.

Bader, V., & Bonotti, M. (2014). Introduction: Parties, partisanship and political theory. *Critical Review of International Social and Political Philosophy, 17*(3), 253–266. Retrieved from https://doi.org/10.1080/13698230.2014.886382

Behn, R. D., & Vaupel, J. W. (1984, Summer). The wasted vote fallacy. *Journal of Policy Analysis and Management, 3*(4), 607–612. Retrieved from https://doi.org/10.2307/3324549

Bolingbroke, H. S. J. (1735). *A dissertation upon parties; in several letters to Caleb D'Anvers, Esq.* (Third ed.). London: H. Haines.

Bolingbroke, H. S. J. (1749). *Letters, on the spirit of patriotism: On the idea of a patriot king: and on the state of parties, at the accession of King George the First.* Dublin: J. Smith.

Brennan, J. (2012). *The ethics of voting.* Princeton: Princeton University Press.

Brennan, J. (2017). *Against democracy.* Princeton: Princeton University Press.

Brennan, J., & Hill, L. (2014). *Compulsory voting: For and against.* Cambridge: Cambridge University Press.

Burke, E. (1769). *Observations on a late state of the nation.* Dublin: A. Leathly, J. Exshaw, B. Grierson, and J. Williams.

Burke, E. (1770). *Thoughts on the cause of the present discontents.* London: J. Dodsley.

Burke, E. (1777). *The political tracts and speeches of Edmund Burke, Esq., member of parliament for the city of Bristol.* Dublin: Printed for W. Whitestone, W. Sleater, J. Williams, W. Wilson,

W. Colles, G. Burnet, J. Exshaw, L. Flin, W. Hallhead, J. Beatty, and M. Mills.

Cartwright, D. E. (2010). *Schopenhauer: A biography*. Cambridge University Press.

Cox, G. W. (1997). *Making votes count: Strategic coordination in the world's electoral systems*. Cambridge: Cambridge University Press.

Crick, F. H. C. (1958). On protein synthesis. In F. K. Sanders (Ed.), *Symposia of the Society for Experimental Biology* (pp. 138–163). Cambridge University Press.

Dalton, R. J., & Klingemann, H.-D. (2009). Overview of political behavior: Political behavior and citizen politics. In R. E. Goodin (Ed.), *The Oxford handbook of political science* (pp. 321–344). Oxford: Oxford University Press.

Dalton, R. J., & Wattenberg, M. P. (Eds.). (2000). *Parties without partisans: Political change in advanced industrial democracies*. Oxford: Oxford University Press.

de la Boétie, E. (1975). *The politics of obedience: The discourse of voluntary servitude*. New York: Free Life Editions.

Destutt de Tracy, A. L. C. (1804). *Élémens d'idéologie. première partie. idéologie proprement dite*. Paris: Courcier.

de Tocqueville, A. (2012). *Democracy in America* (Vol. I; E. Nolla, Ed.). Indianapolis: Liberty Fund.

Disraeli, B. (1883). *Wit and wisdom of Benjamin Disraeli, Earl of Beconsford, collected from his writings and speeches* (New ed.). London: Longmans, Green and Co.

Downs, A. (1957). *An economic theory of democracy*. New York: Harper & Row, Publishers.

Dummett, M. (1997). *Principles of electoral reform*. Oxford: Oxford University Press.

Duverger, M. (1964). *Political parties: Their organization and activity in the modern state* (Third English ed.). London: Methuen & Co. Ltd.

Epstein, L. D. (1967). *Political parties in western democracies*. New York: Praeger Publishers.

Eyma, X. (1862). *La vie dans le nouveau monde*. Paris: Poulet-Malassis.

Farrell, D. M. (2001). *Electoral systems: A comparative introduction*. New York: Palgrave.

Farrell, D. M., & Webb, P. (2000). Political parties as campaign organizations. In R. J. Dalton & M. P. Wattenberg (Eds.), *Parties without partisans: Political change in advanced industrial democracies* (pp. 102–128). Oxford: Oxford University Press.

Follett, M. P. (1918). *The new state: Group organization the solution of popular government.* New York: Longmans, Green and Co.

Follett, M. P. (1924). *Creative experience.* New York: Longmans, Green and Co.

Geertz, C. (1973). Ideology as a cultural system. In *The interpretation of cultures: Selected essays* (pp. 193–233). New York: Basic Books, Inc., Publishers.

Glendon, M. A. (1991). *Rights talk: The impoverishment of political discourse.* New York: The Free Press.

Goodin, R. E. (2008). *Innovating democracy: Democratic theory and practice after the deliberative turn.* Oxford: Oxford University Press.

Gray, F. d. P. (2001). *Simone Weil.* New York: Viking.

Hamilton, A., Madison, J., & Jay, J. (1788). *The Federalist : a collection of essays, written in favour of the new constitution, as agreed upon by the Federal Convention, September 17, 1787* (Vol. 1). New York: J. and A. McLean.

Hendry, R. F. (1995). Realism and progress: Why scientists should be realists. *Royal Institute of Philosophy Supplement, 38,* 53–72.

Hofstadter, R. (1969). *The idea of a party system: The rise of legitimate opposition in the United States, 1780–1840.* Berkeley, Los Angeles, and London: University of California Press.

Hohfeld, W. N. (1913, November). Some fundamental legal conceptions as applied in judicial reasoning. *The Yale Law Journal, 23*(1), 16–59. Retrieved from https://www.jstor.org/stable/785533

Hohfeld, W. N. (1917, June). Fundamental legal conceptions as applied in judicial reasoning. *The Yale Law Journal, 26*(8), 710–770. Retrieved from https://www.jstor.org/stable/786270

Hume, D. (1987). *Essays, moral, political and literary* (E. F. Miller, Ed.). Carmel, Indiana: Liberty Fund.

Janis, I. L. (1982). *Groupthink: Psychological studies of policy decisions and fiascoes* (Second ed.). Boston: Houghton Mifflin Company.

Kant, I. (1965). *Critique of pure reason.* New York: St. Martin's Press.

Kedar, O. (2009). *Voting for policy, not parties: How voters compensate for power sharing.* Cambridge: Cambridge University Press.

Kelsen, H. (2013). *The essence and value of democracy* (N. Urbinati & C. I. Accetti, Eds.). Lanham, Maryland: Rowman & Littlefield Publishers, Inc.

Key, V. O. (1942). *Politics, parties, and pressure groups.* New York: Thomas Y. Crowell Company.

Kierkegaard, S. (1978). *Two ages: The age of revolution and the present age: A literary review* (H. V. Hong & E. H. Hong, Eds.). Princeton: Princeton University Press.

King, A. (1969). Political parties in western democracies: Some sceptical reflections. *Polity, 2*(2), 111-141. Retrieved from https://doi.org/10.2307/3234095

Kirchheimer, O. (1966). The transformation of the Western European party systems. In J. LaPalombara & M. Weiner (Eds.), *Political parties and political development* (pp. 177–200). Princeton: Princeton University Press.

Kroh, M. (2009). The ease of ideological voting: Voter sophistication and party system complexity. In H.-D. Klingemann (Ed.), *The comparative study of electoral systems* (pp. 220–236). Oxford: Oxford University Press.

LaPalombara, J., & Weiner, M. (1966). The origin and development of political parties. In J. LaPalombara & M. Weiner (Eds.), *Political parties and political development* (pp. 3–42). Princeton: Princeton University Press.

Lieber, F. (1876). *Manual of political ethics: designed chiefly for the use of colleges and students at law* (Vol. II). Philadelphia: J. B. Lippincott & Co.

Lijphart, A. (1994). *Electoral systems and party systems: A study of twenty-seven democracies, 1945–1990.* Oxford: Oxford University Press.

Long, A. A. (1986). *Hellenistic philosophy: Stoics, Epicureans, Sceptics* (Second ed.). Berkeley and Los Angeles: University of California Press.

Lorch, M. (2021). *Biochemistry: A very short introduction.* Oxford: Oxford University Press.

Mair, P. (1997). *Party system change: Approaches and interpretations*. Oxford: Clarendon Press.
Mannheim, K. (1960). *Ideology and utopia: An introduction to the sociology of knowledge*. London: Routledge & Kegan Paul Ltd.
Marshall, P. (2010). *Demanding the impossible: A history of anarchism*. Oakland, California: PM Press.
Michels, R. (1915). *Political parties: A sociological study of the oligarchical tendencies of modern democracy*. New York: Hearst's International Library Co.
Mill, J. S. (1977). On liberty. In J. M. Robson (Ed.), *Essays on politics and society* (Vol. XVIII, pp. 213–310). Toronto: University of Toronto Press.
Muirhead, R. (2006). A defense of party spirit. *Perspectives on Politics*, 4(4), 713–727. Retrieved from http://www.jstor.org/stable/20446278
Muirhead, R. (2014). *The promise of party in a polarized age*. Cambridge, Massachusetts: Harvard University Press.
Muirhead, R. (2019). Partisan justification. *Political Theory*, 47(1), pp. 82–89. Retrieved from https://www.jstor.org/stable/26617676
Muirhead, R., & Rosenblum, N. L. (2012, March). The partisan connection. *California Law Review*, 3, 99–112.
Nanetti, R. Y. (1988). Community groups as alternative political organizations in Chicago. In K. Lawson & P. H. Merkl (Eds.), *When parties fail: Emerging alternative organizations* (pp. 170–195). Princeton: Princeton University Press.
Neumann, S. (1956). Toward a comparative study of political parties. In S. Neumann (Ed.), *Modern political parties: Approaches to comparative politics* (pp. 395–421). Chicago & London: The University of Chicago Press.
Nietzsche, F. (2003). *Writings from the late notebooks* (R. Bittner, Ed.). Cambridge: Cambridge University Press.
Nozick, R. (1974). *Anarchy, state, and utopia*. New York: Basic Books, Inc.
Ostrogorski, M. (1902a). *Democracy and the organization of political parties* (Vol. 1). New York: The Macmillan Company.
Ostrogorski, M. (1902b). *Democracy and the organization of political parties* (Vol. 2). New York: The Macmillan Company.
Panebianco, A. (1988). *Political parties: Organization and power*. Cambridge: Cambridge University Press.

Pitkin, H. F. (1967). *The concept of representation.* Berkeley, Los Angeles, and London: University of California Press.

Plato. (1961). *The collected dialogues of Plato* (E. Hamilton & H. Cairns, Eds.). Princeton: Princeton University Press.

Poguntke, T. (1996, April). Anti-party sentiment — conceptual thoughts and empirical evidence: Explorations into a minefield. *European Journal of Political Research, 29,* 319–344.

Pope, A. (1824). *The works of Alexander Pope, Esq. with notes and illustrations by himself and others* (Vol. VIII). London: C. and J. Rivington, et al.

Priest, M. (2014). Party politics and democratic disagreement. *Philosophia, 42*(1), 1–13.

Quagliariello, G. (1996). *Politics without parties: Moisei Ostrogorski and the debate on political parties on the eve of the twentieth century.* Aldershot: Avebury.

Rawls, J. (1999). *A theory of justice* (Revised ed.). Cambridge, Massachusetts: Harvard University Press.

Ressler, M. (2013). *The logic of relativism.* Increasingly Skeptical Publications.

Ressler, M. (2024). *Authentic technological engagement.* Increasingly Skeptical Publications.

Rose, R. (1974). *The problem of party government.* London and Basingstoke: The Macmillan Press Ltd.

Rosenblum, N. L. (2010). *On the side of the angels: An appreciation of parties and partisanship.* Princeton: Princeton University Press.

Ross, D. (1995). *Aristotle.* London and New York: Routledge.

Ross, R. G. (1953). Democracy, party, and politics. *Ethics, 64*(2), 100–125.

Rousseau, J.-J. (1993). *The social contract and the discourses.* New York and Toronto: Alfred A. Knopf.

Sartori, G. (2005). *Parties and party systems: A framework for analysis.* Colchester: ECPR Press.

Scarrow, S. E. (1996, April). Politicians against parties: Anti-party arguments as weapons for change in Germany. *European Journal of Political Research, 29,* 297–317.

Schattschneider, E. E. (2017). *Party government.* London and New York: Routledge.

Seligman, L. G. (1967). Political parties and the recruitment of political leadership. In *Political leadership in industrialized societies* (pp. 294–315). New York: John Wiley & Sons, Inc.

Sextus Empiricus. (2000). *Outlines of scepticism* (J. Annas & J. Barnes, Eds.). Cambridge: Cambridge University Press.

Sidgwick, H. (1891). *The elements of politics.* London and New York: Macmillan and Co.

Sinhababu, N. (2016). In defense of partisanship. In E. Crookston, D. Killoren, & J. Trerise (Eds.), *Ethics in politics: The rights and obligations of individual political agents* (pp. 75–90). New York: Routledge.

Smith, G. (1897). A constitutional misfit. *The North American Review, 164*(486), 625–633. Retrieved from http://www.jstor.org/stable/25118820

Stickney, A. (1890). *The political problem.* New York: Harper & Brothers.

Stirner, M. (1995). *The ego and its own* (D. Leopold, Ed.). Cambridge: Cambridge University Press.

Thoreau, H. D. (2001). Civil disobedience. In *Henry David Thoreau: Collected essays and poems* (pp. 203–234). New York: The Library of America.

Voltaire. (1901). *The works of Voltaire. a contemporary version* (Vol. IV). New York: E. R. Dumont.

Ware, A. (1987). *Citizens, parties, and the state: A reappraisal.* Princeton: Princeton University Press.

Ware, A. (1996). *Political parties and political systems.* Oxford: Oxford University Press.

Washington, G. (1919). *Washington's farewell address.* Washington: Government Printing Office.

Weil, S. (2014). *On the abolition of all political parties.* New York: New York Review Books.

Weinstock, D. (2019). On partisan compromise. *Political Theory, 47*(1), pp. 90–96. Retrieved from https://www.jstor.org/stable/26617677

White, J., & Ypi, L. (2010). Rethinking the modern prince: Partisanship and the democratic ethos. *Political Studies, 58*(4), 809-828. Retrieved from https://doi.org/10.1111/j.1467-9248.2010.00837.x

White, J., & Ypi, L. (2011). On partisan political justification. *American Political Science Review, 105*(2), 381–396.

White, J., & Ypi, L. (2016). *The meaning of partisanship.* Oxford: Oxford University Press.

White, J., & Ypi, L. (2019). Response: The democratic case for partisanship. *Political Theory*, *47*(1), pp. 106–113. Retrieved from https://www.jstor.org/stable/26617679

Wolff, R. P. (1970). *In defense of anarchism*. New York, Evanston, and London: Harper & Row, Publishers.

Zelizer, J. E. (2025). *In defense of partisanship*. New York: Columbia Global Reports.

www.ingramcontent.com/pod-product-compliance
Lightning Source LLC
Chambersburg PA
CBHW030139170426
43199CB00008B/127